MAXIMIZING
THE ARMOR OF GOD

MANUAL

Optimum Vizh-an

Trafford rev. 05/18/2011

 www.trafford.com

North America & international
toll-free: 1 888 232 4444 (USA & Canada)
phone: 250 383 6864 ♦ fax: 812 355 4082

Table of Contents

Dedication

This book is dedicated to
Jesus Christ for Conquering Death,
so that we may live in
His Eternal Presence
forever and ever.

We stand in awe,
with our praises
to you,
for the rest
of our lives.

Thank you
Jesus Christ

Author

Habakkuk

Then the LORD replied:
"Write down the revelation
and make it plain on tablets
so that a herald may run with it.
For the revelation awaits
an appointed time;
it speaks of the end
and will not prove false.
Though it linger,
wait for it;
it will certainly come
and will not delay.

Habakkuk 2:2-3

Preface

At the Advent of Christ establishing: His Church,

MATT 16:18-19. *And I tell you that you are Peter, and on this rock **I will build my** **church,** and the gates of Hades will not overcome it. I will give you the keys of the kingdom of heaven; whatever you bind on earth will be bound in heaven, and whatever you loose on earth will be loosed in heaven.",*

His Bride,

REV 19:7-8. *Let us rejoice and be glad and give Him glory! For the wedding of the Lamb has come, and **His bride** has made herself ready. Fine linen, bright and clean, was given her to wear.",*

His Body,

1 COR 12:22-27. *On the contrary, those parts of the body that seem to be weaker are indispensable, and the parts that we think are less honorable we treat with special honor. And the parts that are unpresentable are treated with special modesty, while our presentable parts need no special treatment. But God has combined the members of the body and has given greater honor to the parts that lacked it, so that there should be no division in the body, but that its parts should have equal concern for each other. If one part suffers, every part suffers with it; if one part is honored, every part rejoices with it. **Now you are the body** **of Christ, and each one of you is a part of it.** EPH 4:12-13. to prepare God's people for works of service, so that the body of Christ may be built up until we all reach unity in the faith and in the knowledge of the Son of God and become mature, attaining to the whole measure of the fullness of Christ.,*

Christ baptized His new
Church/Bride/Body in the Holy Spirit...

MATT 3:11. *"I baptize you with water for repentance. But after me will come one who is more powerful than I, whose sandals I am not fit to carry. **He will** **baptize you with the Holy Spirit and with fire.** ACTS 1:8. But **you will receive** **power** when the Holy Spirit comes on you; and you will be my witnesses in Jerusalem, and in all Judea and Samaria, and to the ends of the earth." LUKE 12:11-12. "When you are brought before synagogues, rulers and authorities, do* *not worry about how you will defend yourselves or what you will say, **for the Holy Spirit will teach you** at that time what you should say." 1 COR 12:7-11. Now to each one the manifestation of the Spirit is given for the common good. To one there is given through the Spirit the message of wisdom, to another the message of knowledge by means of the same Spirit, to another faith by the same Spirit, to another gifts of healing by that one Spirit, to another miraculous powers, to another prophecy,to another distinguishing between spirits, to another speaking in different kinds of tongues, and to still another the interpretation of tongues. **All these are the work of one and the same Spirit,** and he gives them to each one, just as he determines. HEB 2:4. God also testified to it by signs, wonders and various miracles, and gifts of the **Holy Spirit distributed according to his will.** 1 COR 14:12. So it is with you. Since you are eager to have spiritual gifts, try to **excel in gifts that build up the church.***

to establish it, to sustain it and to multiply it, until and beyond all of the kingdom's have become His.

DAN 2:44-45. *"In the time of those kings, the God of heaven will set up a kingdom that will never be destroyed, nor will it be left to another people. **It will crush all those kingdoms and bring them to an end, but it will itself endure forever.***

As the Church/Bride/Body/Kingdom of Christ started to expand and convert cultures, governments and religions, those who were threatened by Christ establishing His Church/Bride/Body/Kingdom, fought back. While others organized in hopes of ridding themselves from this new phenomena for centuries.

ACTS 7:57-8:3. *At this they **covered their ears and, yelling at the top of their voices, they all rushed at him, dragged him out of the city and began to stone him.** Meanwhile, the witnesses laid their clothes at the feet of a young man named Saul. While they were stoning him, Stephen prayed, "Lord Jesus, receive my spirit." Then he fell on his knees and cried out, "Lord, do not hold this sin against them." When he had said this, he fell asleep. ACTS 8:1. And Saul was there, giving approval to his death. **On that day a great persecution broke out against the church at Jerusalem,** and all except the apostles were scattered throughout Judea and Samaria. Godly men buried Stephen and mourned deeply for him. But **Saul began to destroy the church. Going from house to house, he dragged off men and women and put them in prison.***

However it had the opposite effect.

ACTS 8:4-8. *Those who had been scattered preached the word wherever they went.* *Philip went down to a city in Samaria and proclaimed the Christ there. When the crowds heard Philip and saw the miraculous signs he did, they all paid close attention to what he said. With shrieks, evil spirits came out of many, and many paralytics and cripples were healed.* *So there was great joy in that city.*

During this birthing time of the Church/Bride/Body/ Kingdom of Christ, the weaker believers needed revelations, that would encourage them to withstand the temptations of giving into the opposition.

1 COR 3:1-4 3:1. *Brothers, I could not address you as spiritual but as worldly- mere infants in Christ. I gave you milk, not solid food, for you were not yet ready for it. Indeed, you are still not ready.* *You are still worldly. For since there is jealousy and quarreling among you, are you not worldly? Are you not acting like mere men? For when one says, "I follow Paul," and another, "I follow Apollos," are you not mere men?*

During this time, Paul makes a correlation of spiritual matters to physical matters. Not that the spiritual matters were reduced to the same futile purposes, but in hopes of at least understanding why and how the physical matters were to be used effectively. These new metaphors became the new common language, that would help new believers understand how spiritual concepts can be used as effective spiritual weapons against their unseen enemies. This is how Paul puts it,

EPH 6:10-18. *Finally, be strong in the Lord and in his mighty power. Put on the full armor of God so that you can take your stand against the devil's schemes. For our struggle is not against flesh and blood, but against the rulers, against the authorities, against the powers of this dark world and against the spiritual forces of evil in the heavenly realms. Therefore put on the full armor of God, so that when the day of evil comes, you may be able to stand your ground, and after you have done everything, to stand. Stand firm then, with the belt of truth buckled around your waist, with the breastplate of righteousness in place, and with your feet fitted with the readiness that comes from the gospel of peace. In addition to all this, take up the shield of faith, with which you can extinguish all the flaming arrows of the evil one. Take the helmet of salvation and the sword of the Spirit, which is the word of God. And pray in the Spirit on all occasions with all kinds of prayers and requests. With this in mind, be alert and always keep on praying for all the saints.*

In Romans and 2 Corinthians, Paul makes more references to armor, weapons and the correlation of how these spiritual truths can be applied to suppress spiritual enemies.

ROM 13:12. *The night is nearly over, the day is almost here. So let us put aside the deeds of darkness and **put on the armor of light.** In 2 COR 10:3-5. For though we live in the world, we do not wage war as the world does. **The weapons we fight with are not the weapons of the world.** On the contrary, **they have divine power** to demolish strongholds. We demolish arguments and every pretension that sets itself up against the knowledge of God, and we take captive every thought to make it obedient to Christ.*

With faith, patience and the leading of the Holy Spirit, they lived to see the Holy Spirit be poured out on the Gentiles as well.

ACTS 10:45. *The circumcised believers who had come with Peter were astonished that the gift of **the Holy Spirit had been poured out even on the Gentiles.***

Those who were threaten, by this new phenomena, ended up waging a sober deadening blow to Christ's Church/Bride/Body. Most of the witnesses that lived to see Christ launch His Church/Bride/Body/Kingdom, had died deaths that would send chills up the spines of newer generations seeking eternal life. Centuries came and gone. Each century ending like the last, with the Church/Bride/Body/Kingdom of Christ still intimidated by the stories told on how first century believers died as martyrs. Even though at large she was intimidated, the Holy Spirit continued(s) to expand Christ's Church/Bride/Body/Kingdom. Some expansions are easier to see than others. Some hanging on by a thread. However, like a child, this was only for a season.
For we read in,

JOEL 2:27-32. *Then you will know that I am in Israel, that I am the LORD your God, and that there is no other; **never again will my people be shamed.** 'And afterward, **I will pour out my Spirit on all people.** Your sons and daughters will prophesy, your old men will dream dreams, your young men will see visions. Even on my servants, both men and women, **I will pour out my Spirit in those days.** I will show wonders in the heavens and on the earth, blood and fire and billows of smoke. The sun will be turned to darkness and the moon to blood before the coming of the great and dreadful day of the LORD. And everyone who calls on the name of the LORD will be saved; for on Mount Zion and in Jerusalem there will be deliverance, as the LORD has said, among the survivors whom the LORD calls.*

If we look at this in the eyes of a world with no absolutes, we see hypocrisy, chaos and death. If we look at this in the eyes of the Spirit and in Truth, we see an epic war between death and life being played out. God's word tells us this epic war started in heaven. Lucifer and his hordes were removed from heaven and banished to the earth. This would be the first major battle between death and life.

REV 12:7-9. **And there was war in heaven.** *Michael and his angels fought against the dragon, and the dragon and his angels fought back. But he was not strong enough, and they lost their place in heaven. **The great dragon was hurled down-that ancient serpent called the devil, or Satan, who leads the whole world astray.** He was hurled to the earth, and his angels with him.*

EZEK 28:16-19. *Through your widespread trade you were filled with violence, and you sinned. So I drove you in disgrace from the mount of God, and I expelled you, **O guardian cherub, from among the fiery stones. Your heart became proud on account of your beauty, and you corrupted your wisdom because of your splendor. So I threw you to the earth;** I made a spectacle of you before kings. By your many sins and dishonest trade you have desecrated your sanctuaries. So I made a fire come out from you, and it consumed you, and I reduced you to ashes on the ground in the sight of all who were watching. All the nations who knew you are appalled at you; you have come to a horrible end and will be no more."'*

Lucifer and his hordes regrouped, plotted and orchestrated the fall of man. This is the second major battle between death and life.

REV 12:13. **When the dragon saw that he had been hurled to the earth, he pursued the woman** *who had given birth to the male child. GEN 3:1-5. Now **the serpent** was more crafty than any of the wild animals the LORD God had* made. *He said to the woman, "Did God really say, 'You must not eat from any tree in the garden'?"* The woman said to the serpent, "We may eat fruit from the trees in the garden, but God did say, 'You must not eat fruit from the tree that is in the middle of the garden, and you must not touch it, or you will die.'" "You will not surely die," **the serpent said to the woman. "For God knows that when you eat of it your eyes will be opened, and you will be like God, knowing good and evil."**

In essence, man sells his birth right of dominion over all, for an eye opening experience, which has led him down the path of hypocrisy, chaos and death. When man yielded his dominion, Lucifer and his hordes established, assumed places of dominion on the earth, tormenting man until the flood in Noah's day.

REV 12:12. *Therefore rejoice, you heavens and you who dwell in them!* **But woe to the earth and the sea, because the devil has gone down to you! He is filled with fury, because he knows that his time is short."** GEN 6:11-14. *Now the earth was corrupt in God's sight and was full of violence.* **God saw how corrupt the earth had become,** *for all the people on earth had corrupted their ways. So* **God said to Noah, "I am going to put an end to all people,** *for the earth is filled with violence because of them. I am surely going to destroy both them and the earth.*

After God flooded the earth as He stated, this would be considered the third major battle between death and life. After the flood to Christ, this epic war continued more or less the same, with no major noted battles.

After Christ's death and resurrection, He set up His Church/Bride/Body/Kingdom and baptized those who believed with the Holy Spirit, the Comforter. His setup and launch was extremely successful, effective and multiplying at an aggressive speed.

DAN 2:44-45. *"In the time of those kings,* **the God of heaven will set up a kingdom that will never be destroyed,** *nor will it be left to another people. It will crush all those kingdoms and bring them to an end, but it will itself endure forever. MATT 11:12-13. (Jesus) From the days of John the Baptist until now,* **the kingdom of heaven has been forcefully advancing,** *and forceful men lay hold of it. JOHN 12:30-32 Jesus said, "This voice was for your benefit, not mine.*

Now is the time for judgment on this world; now the prince of this world will be driven out. ACTS 4:31. *After they prayed, the place where they were meeting was shaken. And **they were all filled with the Holy Spirit and spoke the word of God boldly.** ACTS 6:7. So the word of God spread. The **number of disciples** in Jerusalem **increased rapidly**, and **a large number of priests became obedient to the faith.** ACTS 12:24. But the **word of God continued to increase and spread.***

Lucifer and his hordes suffered huge blows. It had looked as thought the gates of hell would not prevail. Lucifer regrouped, plotted and orchestrated spine chilling deaths, to all the key leaders/witnesses of Christ's Death and Resurrection. This would be considered the fourth major battle between death and life.

In the year which I write this, the fifth and sixth major battles have not occurred yet. The fifth major battle is best described by

REV 19:11-20:3. ***I saw heaven standing open and there before me was a white horse, whose rider is called Faithful and True.*** *With justice he judges and makes war. His eyes are like blazing fire, and on his head are many crowns. He has a name written on him that no one knows but he himself. **He is dressed in a robe dipped in blood, and his name is the Word of God. The armies of heaven were following him, riding on white horses and dressed in fine linen, white and clean.** Out of his mouth comes a sharp sword with which to strike down the nations. "He will rule them with an iron scepter." He treads the winepress of the fury of the wrath of God Almighty. On his robe and on his thigh he has this name written: KING OF KINGS AND LORD OF LORDS. And I saw an angel standing in the sun, who cried in a loud voice to all the birds flying in midair, "Come, gather together for the great supper of God, so that you may eat the flesh of kings, generals, and mighty men, of horses and their riders, and the flesh of all people, free and slave, small and great." **Then I saw the beast and the kings of the earth and their armies gathered together to make war against the rider on the horse and his army. But the beast was captured, and with him the false prophet who had performed the miraculous signs on his behalf.** With these signs he had deluded those who had received the mark of the beast and worshiped his image. **The two of them were thrown alive into the fiery lake of burning sulfur.** The rest of them were killed with the sword that came out of the mouth of the rider on the horse, and all the birds gorged themselves on their flesh. REV 20 20:1. And I saw an angel coming down out of heaven, having the key to the Abyss and holding in his hand a great chain. **He seized the dragon, that ancient serpent, who is*** *the devil, or Satan, and bound him for a thousand years. He threw him into the Abyss, and locked and sealed it over him, to keep him from deceiving the nations anymore **until the thousand years were ended. After that, he must be set free for a short time.***

Combined, with References of Christ coming back, to a Bride who makes herself ready.

REV 19:6-8 *6. Then I heard what sounded like a great multitude, like the roar of rushing waters and like loud peals of thunder, shouting: "Hallelujah! For our Lord God Almighty reigns. Let us rejoice and be glad and give him glory! For the wedding of the Lamb has come, and **his bride has made herself ready.** Fine linen, bright and clean, was given her to wear." - Fine linen stands for the righteous acts of the saints. EPH 5:25-28. Husbands, love your wives, just as Christ loved the church and gave himself up for her to **make her holy, cleansing her by the washing with water through the word, and to present her to himself as a radiant church,** without stain or wrinkle or any other blemish, but holy and blameless.*

Christ is a Warrior/King coming for His Warrior Bride/Queen.

ROM 8:5. *Those who live according to the sinful nature have their minds set on what that nature desires; but those who live in accordance with the Spirit have their minds set on what the Spirit desires. REV 5:10. And hast made us unto our God kings and priests: and we shall reign on the earth.*

With these three explosive variables coming together; Christ coming back as King, A Bride/Queen who makes herself ready and Lucifer with his hordes fighting with all their might - determined to avoid being locked up for a thousands years, will make this the fifth major battle, the second to mother of all battles.

The sixth and last major battle is so huge, it dwarfs all the previous battles combined plus many times over.

It involves everyone and everything in all the heavens.

REV 20:7-12. ***When the thousand years are over, Satan will be released from his prison and will go out to deceive the nations in the four corners of the earth-***

Gog and Magog-to gather them for battle. **In number they are like the sand on the seashore. They marched across the breadth of the earth** *and surrounded the camp of God's people, the city he loves. But fire came down from heaven and devoured them. And the devil, who deceived them, was thrown into the lake of burning sulfur, where the beast and the false prophet had been thrown. They will be tormented day and night for ever and ever. Then I saw a great white throne and him who was seated on it. Earth and sky fled from his presence, and there was no place for them.* 2 PET 3:10. *But the day of the Lord will come like a thief.* **The heavens will disappear with a roar; the elements will be destroyed by fire, and the earth and everything in it will be laid bare.** ZEPH 1:18. *Neither their silver nor their gold will be able to save them on the day of the LORD's wrath. In the fire of his jealousy* **the whole world will be consumed, for he will make a sudden end of all who live in the earth."** AMOS 5:20. **Will not the day of the LORD be darkness,** *not light-pitch-dark, without a ray of brightness?* JOEL 2:1-3. *Blow the trumpet in Zion; sound the alarm on my holy hill. Let all who live in the land tremble, for the day of the LORD is coming. It is close at hand- a day of darkness and gloom, a day of clouds and blackness.* **Like dawn spreading across the mountains a large and mighty army comes, such as never was of old nor ever will be in ages to come.** *Before them fire devours, behind them a flame blazes. Before them the land is like the garden of Eden, behind them, a desert waste- nothing escapes them.* ISAIAH 13:9-13. *See, the day of the LORD is coming — a cruel day, with wrath and fierce anger — to make the land desolate and destroy the sinners within it. The stars of heaven and their constellations will not show their light. The rising sun will be darkened and the moon will not give its light.* **I will punish the world for its evil, the wicked for their sins. I will put an end to the arrogance of the haughty and will humble the pride of the ruthless.** *I will make man scarcer than pure gold, more rare than the gold of Ophir. Therefore I will make the heavens tremble; and the earth will shake from its place at the wrath of the LORD Almighty, in the day of his burning anger.* ISAIAH 13:6-8. **Wail, for the day of the LORD is near; it will come like destruction from the Almighty.** *Because of this, all hands will go limp, every man's heart will melt. Terror will seize them, pain and anguish will grip them; they will writhe like a woman in labor. They will look aghast at each other, their faces aflame.*

This "Big Picture" view on the War between Life and Death, allows us to put our personal challenges into a more balanced perspective.

If your healthy, blessed and find no purpose or use for these words, tools and weapons then consider if God is calling you to arms, to establish His Kingdom, by setting the captives free and defending those who can not defend themselves.

EZEK 22:30. And *I sought for a man among them, that should make up the hedge, and stand in the gap before Me for the land.* ISAIAH 61:1. *The Spirit of the Lord GOD is upon me; because the LORD hath anointed me to preach good tidings unto the meek; **he hath sent me to bind up the brokenhearted, to proclaim liberty to the captives, and the opening of the prison to them that are bound;** KJV PSALMS 82:3-4. **Defend the poor and fatherless: do justice to the afflicted and needy. Deliver the poor and needy: rid them out of the hand of the wicked.** KJV PROV 31:8-9. **"Speak up for those who cannot speak for themselves,** for the rights of all who are destitute. Speak up and judge fairly; defend the rights of the poor and needy."*

As Paul made the attempt and correlation on how to use spiritual truths, to overcome spiritual enemies, so we to with this manual.

Warriors

Two warriors face to face are battling against each other for their very own survival. Both are using the finest armor a warrior can own. One warrior will win. One warrior will lose... Who will it be?

On the surface both warriors appear to be equally matched. Both tested and tried by the best of disciplines. Both look as though neither will lose... How can this be?

Both warriors can execute precision attack and counter attacks that are predictably synchronized. One is for life. One is for death. The *Warrior for Life* lives to enjoy life. But before he can maximize his enjoyment of life he must first kill the Warrior of Death. The *Warrior of Death* lives to enjoy death. But before he can maximize his enjoyment of death he must first kill the Warrior of Life. Both warriors will have no peace until each has victory over the other... When can this be?

The Warrior of Life enjoyed life without death, until the Warrior of Death took his first victim of life. From that moment on, the Warrior of Life had dedicated His life in doing battle against the Warrior of Death, until the Warrior of Death was dead. The Warrior of Life had no peace as long as the Warrior of Death was alive. The period of time with no peace was as long as it took the Warrior of Life to kill the Warrior of Death.

The Warrior of Death enjoyed Death as long as the Warrior of Life was Alive. The Warrior of Death had Peace as long as the Warrior of Life was Alive. The Period of Time with Peace was as long as it took the Warrior of Death to kill the Warrior of Life.

The Goal of the Warrior of Life is to Kill the Warrior of Death as soon as possible. The sooner the Warrior of Life kills the Warrior of Death the sooner the Warrior of Life can enjoy Life again without Death. The Warrior of Life is consumed in eradicating death so that life can maximize it's enjoyment of life.

The Warrior of Life can enjoy Life without Death.

The Warrior of Death can not enjoy Death without Life. For the enjoyment of the Warrior of Death is in the killing of Life and when the killing of Life is all done then so too is the enjoyment of the Warrior of Death in killing Life.

So the Goal of the Warrior of Death is to Maximize the killing of just enough Life, without killing all of Life, so that Life can reproduce enough Life, so that the Warrior of Death never runs out of Life to kill.

The Warrior of Death needs life more than life needs death. If there is no more life, death cannot maximize it's enjoyment of killing/death.

The Warrior of Life does not fear Death. The Warrior of Death does not fear Life. Both will go to the ends of creation to kill each another.

Both are searching for protégées that will dedicate their lives for the same cause. After countless years of searching, both of them have found themselves in the battle field of your mind. Both solicit you to choose their side. The Warrior of

Life doesn't force anyone to join his cause. The Warrior of Death will find out who is the most meaningful person to you in your life and then proceed to kill them. The Warrior of Death hopes that the bitterness of the loved one's death, will motivate you to either kill yourself and or try to hurt others. If you choose to resist then you will be in the greatest battle of your life. If you choose to participate then you will be in the greatest battle of your life. Choose wisely.

Protection

Our protection is only as good as we can use it. We can load ourselves up with all the latest weaponry to do battle with, but if we don't know how to use it, if we don't practice with it and if we don't know how to maximize it, then our protection is worthless.

PROTECTION CHOICE - ACCOUNTABIILITY:

MATT 26:52-54. *"Put your sword back in its place,"* Jesus said to him, **"for all who draw the sword will die by the sword.** *Do you think I cannot call on my Father, and he will at once put at my disposal more than twelve legions of angels? But how then would the Scriptures be fulfilled that say it must happen in this way?"*

ECCL 9:18. **Wisdom is better than weapons of war,** *but one sinner destroys much good.*

PROTECTION CHOICE - BY EXPERIENCE:

SAM 17:38-40. *Then Saul dressed David in his own tunic. He put a coat of armor on him and a bronze helmet on his head. David fastened on his sword over the tunic and tried walking around, because he was not used to them. "I cannot go in these," he said to Saul, "because I am not used to them." So he took them off.* **Then he took his staff in his hand, chose five smooth stones from the stream, put them in the pouch of his shepherd's bag and, with his sling in his hand, approached the Philistine.**

PROTECTION CHOICE - MIND FRAME:

1 SAM 17:45-47. *David said to the Philistine, "You come against me with sword and spear and javelin,* **but I come against you in the name of the LORD Almighty, the God of the armies of Israel, whom you have defied.** *This day the LORD will hand you over to me, and I'll strike you down and cut off your head. Today I will give the carcasses of the Philistine army to the birds of the air and the beasts of the earth, and the whole world will know that there is a God in Israel. All those gathered here will know that it is not by sword or spear that the LORD saves; for the battle is the LORD's, and he will give all of you into our hands."*

4

MATT 10:27-28. ***Do not be afraid of those who kill the body but cannot kill the soul.*** *Rather, be afraid of the One who can destroy both soul and body in hell.*

ZECH 4:6. *So he said to me, "This is the word of the LORD to Zerubbabel: 'Not by might nor by power,* ***but by my Spirit,' says the LORD Almighty.***

PROTECTION CHOICE - MAXIMUM IMPACT:

HEB 4:12. ***For the word of God is living and active. Sharper than any double-edged sword,*** *it penetrates even to dividing soul and spirit, joints and marrow; it judges the thoughts and attitudes of the heart.*

PROV 18:21. ***The tongue has the power of life and death,*** *and those who love it will eat its fruit.*

PROV 22:9. ***He that hath a bountiful eye shall be blessed;*** *for he giveth of his bread to the poor. KJV*

MATT 12:36-37. *But I tell you that men will have to give account on the day of judgment for every careless word they have spoken.* ***For by your words you will be acquitted,*** *and by your words you will be condemned."*

MATT 17:20. *He replied, "Because you have so little faith. I tell you the truth,* ***if you have faith as small as a mustard seed, you can say to this mountain, 'Move from here to there' and it will move.*** *Nothing will be impossible for you."*

LUKE 10:18-20. *He replied, "I saw Satan fall like lightning from heaven.* ***I have given you authority to trample on snakes and scorpions and to overcome all the power of the enemy; nothing will harm you.*** *However, do not rejoice that the spirits submit to you, but rejoice that your names are written in heaven."*

MARK 16:15-18. *He said to them, "Go into all the world and preach the good news to all creation. Whoever believes and is baptized will be saved, but whoever does not believe will be condemned.* ***And these signs will accompany those who believe: In my name they will drive out demons; they will speak in new tongues; they will pick up snakes with their hands; and when they drink deadly poison, it will not hurt them at all; they will place their hands on sick people, and they will get well."***

PROTECTION CHOICE - SUMMARY:

This is our fork in the road decision. We can either decide to solve our conflicts by our might or by God's Spirit. Each will require faith to pursue. A faith that believes the solution will bring peace to the conflict. Both choices are very challenging to master. Both will require dedication and accountability. This manual pursues solving conflicts/challenges spiritually.

Preparation

Our preparation is only as good as the protection we choose and how we practice with it.

David with bear, lion...

1 SAM 17:33-37. *Saul replied, "You are not able to go out against this Philistine and fight him; you are only a boy, and he has been a fighting man from his youth." But David said to Saul, "Your servant has been keeping his father's sheep. When a lion or a bear came and carried off a sheep from the flock, I went after it, struck it and rescued the sheep from its mouth. When it turned on me, I seized it by its hair, struck it and killed it. **Your servant has killed both the lion and the bear;** this uncircumcised Philistine will be like one of them, because he has defied the armies of the living God. The LORD who delivered me from the paw of the lion and the paw of the bear will deliver me from the hand of this Philistine."*

We can do all the drill routines we think we need to do before battle, but if we don't know the right mindset, if we can't persevere and if we can't change our tactics at the last minute then our preparation is worthless.

PREPARATION - CRITERIA:

1 SAM 16:7. *But the LORD said to Samuel, "Do not consider his appearance or his height, for I have rejected him. The LORD does not look at the things man looks at. Man looks at the outward appearance, but **the LORD looks at the heart.**"*

ROM 12:14. *Bless those who persecute you; **bless and do not curse.***

REV 3:15-17. ***I know your deeds,** that you are neither cold nor hot. **I wish you were either one or the other!** So, because you are lukewarm-neither hot nor cold-I am about to spit you out of my mouth.*

MATT 5:37. ***But let your communication be, Yea, yea; Nay, nay: for whatsoever is more than these cometh of evil.** KJV*

PREPARATION - COST ACCOUNTABILITY:

LUKE 14:28-33. *"Suppose one of you wants to build a tower. Will he not first sit down and estimate the cost to see if he has enough money to complete it? For if he lays the foundation and is not able to finish it, everyone who sees it will ridicule him, saying, 'This fellow began to build and was not able to finish.'* "Or suppose a king is about to go to war against another king. Will he not first sit down and consider whether he is able with ten thousand men to oppose the one coming against him with twenty thousand? If he is not able, he will send a delegation while the other is still a long way off and will ask for terms of peace. In the same way, any of you who does not give up everything he has cannot be my disciple.

This type of warfare can not be bought and can not be used independently of God. Simon tried to buy it from Peter.

ACTS 8:18-24. When Simon saw that the Spirit was given at the laying on of the apostles' hands, he offered them money and said, "Give me also this ability so that everyone on whom I lay my hands may receive the Holy Spirit." **Peter answered: "May your money perish with you, because you thought you could buy the gift of God with money!** You have no part or share in this ministry, because your heart is not right before God. Repent of this wickedness and pray to the Lord. Perhaps he will forgive you for having such a thought in your heart. For I see that you are full of bitterness and captive to sin." Then Simon answered, "Pray to the Lord for me so that nothing you have said may happen to me."

PREPARATION - MIND FRAME:

2 TIM 1:7. *For God did not give us a spirit of timidity, but a spirit of power, of love and of self-discipline.*

JOSH 1:7-8. Do not let this **Book of the Law** depart from your mouth; **meditate on it day and night, so that you may be careful to do everything written in it.** Then you will be prosperous and successful.

JOSH 1:9. Have I not commanded you? Be strong and courageous. **Do not be terrified; do not be discouraged, for the LORD your God will be with you wherever you go."**

MARK 11:24. Therefore I say unto you, **What things so ever ye desire, when ye pray, believe that ye receive them, and ye shall have them.** KJV

HEB 11:6. **But without faith it is impossible to please him**: for he that cometh to God must believe that he is, and that he is a rewarder of them that diligently seek him. KJV

PHIL 4:6. **Be careful for nothing**; but in every thing by prayer and supplication with thanksgiving let your requests be made known unto God. KJV

1 JOHN 5:14-15. **And this is the confidence that we have in him,** that, if we ask any thing according to his will, he hears us: And if we know that he heasr us, whatsoever we ask, we know that we have the petitions we desired of him. KJV

ECCL 5:2. **Be not rash with thy mouth, and let not thine heart be hasty to utter any thing before God:** for God is in heaven, and thou upon earth: therefore let thy words be few. KJV

EPH 6:11-13. **For our struggle is not against flesh and blood, but against the rulers, against the authorities, against the powers of this dark world and against the spiritual forces of evil in the heavenly realms.**

EPH 4:21-24. **You were taught, with regard to your former way of life, to put off your old self, which is being corrupted by its deceitful desires;** to be made new in the attitude of your minds; and to put on the new self, created to be like God in true righteousness and holiness.

2 COR 5:16-17. Therefore, **if anyone is in Christ, he is a new creation;** the old has gone, the new has come!

2 PET 1:5-11. For this very reason, **make every effort to add to your faith goodness; and to goodness, knowledge; and to knowledge, self-control; and to self-control, perseverance; and to perseverance, godliness; and to godliness, brotherly kindness; and to brotherly kindness, love.** For if you possess these qualities in increasing measure, they will keep you from being ineffective and unproductive in your knowledge of our Lord Jesus Christ. But if anyone does not have them, he is nearsighted and blind, and has forgotten that he has been cleansed from his past sins. Therefore, my brothers, be all the more eager to make your calling and election sure. For if you do these things, you will never fall, and you will receive a rich welcome into the eternal kingdom of our Lord and Savior Jesus Christ.

PSALMS 13:2. How long must I wrestle with my thoughts and every day have sorrow in my heart? **How long will my enemy triumph over me?**

1 PET 2:11-12. Dear friends, **I urge you,** as aliens and strangers in the world, **to abstain from sinful desires, which war against your soul.** Live such good lives among the pagans that, though they accuse you of doing wrong, they may see your good deeds and glorify God on the day he visits us.

GAL 6:8. **The one who sows to please his sinful nature, from that nature will reap destruction;** the one who sows to please the Spirit, from the Spirit will reap eternal life.

ROM 7:21-25. So I find this law at work: When I want to do good, evil is right there with me. For in my inner being I delight in God's law; but **I see another law at work in the members of my body, waging war against the law of my mind and making me a prisoner of the law of sin at work within my members.** What a wretched man I am! Who will rescue me from this body of death? Thanks be to God-through Jesus Christ our Lord!

ROM 8:13-17. **For if you live according to the sinful nature, you will die; but if by the Spirit you put to death the misdeeds of the body, you will live,** *because those who are led by the Spirit of God are sons of God. For you did not receive a spirit that makes you a slave again to fear, but you received the Spirit of sonship. And by him we cry, "Abba, Father." The Spirit himself testifies with our spirit that we are God's children. Now if we are children, then we are heirs-heirs of God and co-heirs with Christ, if indeed we share in his sufferings in order that we may also share in his glory.*

The prayer of a righteous man is powerful and effective. JAMES 5:16. Our righteousness is as filthy rags before Him. ISAIAH 64:6. But through our belief that Christ dwells within our hearts by faith, EPH 3:17, God sees Christ's righteousness in us. Now, through Christ we can boldly go into the throne room of God. HEB 4:16. Then use our tongues PROV 18:21. (the sword - the Word) against/refute ISAIAH 54:17 our unseen enemies, by taking a stand in who we are in Christ.

PREPARATION -
PERSONAL STATUS ACCOUNTABLITY:

LUKE 6:43-45. **"No good tree bears bad fruit, nor does a bad tree bear good fruit. Each tree is recognized by its own fruit.** *People do not pick figs from thorn bushes, or grapes from briers. The good man brings good things out of the good stored up in his heart, and the evil man brings evil things out of the evil stored up in his heart. For out of the overflow of his heart his mouth speaks.*

MATT 6:22-23. *"The eye is the lamp of the body.* **If your eyes are good, your whole body will be full of light.** *But if your eyes are bad, your whole body will be full of darkness. If then the light within you is darkness, how great is that darkness!*

MATT 6:20-21. *But store up for yourselves treasures in heaven, where moth and rust do not destroy, and where thieves do not break in and steal.* **For where your treasure is, there your heart will be also.**

Jer 34:12-35:1. *Then the word of the LORD came to Jeremiah: "This is what the LORD, the God of Israel, says: I made a covenant with your forefathers when I brought them out of Egypt, out of the land of slavery. I said, 'Every seventh year each of you must free any fellow Hebrew who has sold himself to you. After he has served you six years, you must let him go free.'* **Your fathers, however, did not listen to me or pay attention to me. Recently you repented and did what is right in my sight:** *Each of you proclaimed freedom to his countrymen. You even made a covenant before me in the house that bears my Name.* **But**

now you have turned around and profaned my name; each of you has taken back the male and female slaves you had set free to go where they wished. You have forced them to become your slaves again. "Therefore, this is what the LORD says: You have not obeyed me; you have not proclaimed freedom for your fellow countrymen. **So I now proclaim 'freedom' for you, declares the LORD — 'freedom' to fall by the sword, plague and famine.** I will make you abhorrent to all the kingdoms of the earth. The men who have violated my covenant and have not fulfilled the terms of the covenant they made before me, I will treat like the calf they cut in two and then walked between its pieces. The leaders of Judah and Jerusalem, the court officials, the priests and all the people of the land who walked between the pieces of the calf, I will hand over to their enemies who seek their lives. Their dead bodies will become food for the birds of the air and the beasts of the earth. "I will hand Zedekiah king of Judah and his officials over to their enemies who seek their lives, to the army of the king of Babylon, which has withdrawn from you. I am going to give the order, declares the LORD, and I will bring them back to this city. They will fight against it, take it and burn it down. And I will lay waste the towns of Judah so no one can live there."

1 SAM 13:7-14. *Saul remained at Gilgal and all the troops with him were quaking with fear. He waited seven days, the time set by Samuel; but Samuel did not come to Gilgal, and Saul's men began to scatter. So he said, "Bring me the burnt offering and the fellowship offerings." And* **Saul offered up the burnt offering. Just as he finished making the offering, Samuel arrived, and Saul went out to greet him. "What have you done?"** *asked Samuel. Saul replied, "When I saw that the men were scattering, and that you did not come at the set time, and that the Philistines were assembling at Micmash, I thought, ' Now the Philistines ill come down against me at Gilgal, and I have not sought the LORD's favor.' So I felt compelled to offer the burnt offering."* **"You acted foolishly," Samuel said. "You have not kept the command the LORD your God gave you; if you had, he would have established your kingdom over Israel for all time.** *But now your kingdom will not endure; the LORD has sought out a man after his own heart and appointed him leader of his people, because you have not kept the LORD's command."*

Matt 12:35-37. **The good man brings good things out of the good stored up in him**, and the evil man brings evil things out of the evil stored up in him. But I tell you that men will have to give account on the day of judgment for every careless word they have spoken.

Prov 28:13. **he who conceals his sins does not prosper** but whosoever   confesses and renounces them find mercy.

Heb 4:13. **Nothing in all creation is hidden from God's sight.** Everything is uncovered and laid bare before the eyes of him to whom we must give account.

PREPARATION - SUMMARY:

How well do we know our adversary? Do we know him well enough to repeatedly predict his moves? How come he knows us so much better than we know ourselves? Why does he know which one of our buttons to push, to carry out his goals?

Death can only confuse, block and or disrupt but never control or create or demise a new ending. He doesn't have the means or the ends (tools) to get the job done.

Death's only hope in getting what he wants is through our hands. This will continue as long as we allow it, until we discover our true potential. The day we choose to unlock this true potential, is the day death will be empty handed, without a kingdom and alone.

In Christ, we have the opportunity to know the truth. Our true potential. A truth that reveals the end results of our disobedience and obedience. What is sown is reaped. We plant corn seeds, we get corn plants.

Performance

Our performance is only as good as the protection we choose, how we practice with it and the results we get. We can do all the performance comparison results we think we'll need to increase our odds in doing battle; but if we don't know the purpose of why we're going to battle, if we don't stay focus on eliminating our enemies and if we don't listen to God's voice regarding the battle then our performance is worthless.

PERFORMANCE - TESTING:

MARK 9:26-29. *And the spirit cried, and rent him sore, and came out of him: and he was as one dead; insomuch that many said, He is dead. But Jesus took him by the hand, and lifted him up; and he arose. And when he was come into the house,* **his disciples asked him privately, Why could not we cast him out? And he said unto them, This kind can come forth by nothing, but by prayer and fasting.** *KJV*

ACTS 19:15-19. **[One day] the evil spirit answered them, "Jesus I know, and I know about Paul, but who are you?" Then the man who had the evil spirit jumped on them and overpowered them all.** *He gave them such a beating that they ran out of the house naked and bleeding. When this became known to the Jews and Greeks living in Ephesus, they were all seized with fear, and the name of the Lord Jesus was held in high honor. Many of those who believed now came and openly confessed their evil deeds.*

PERFORMANCE - MAXIMIZE SYNCRONIZING THE TIMING:

ECCL 3:1-8. **There is a time for everything, and a season for every activity under heaven:** *a time to be born and a time to die, a time to plant and a time to uproot, a time to kill and a time to heal, a time to tear down and a time to build, a time to weep and a time to laugh, a time to mourn and a time to dance, a time to scatter stones and a time to gather them, a time to embrace and a time to refrain, a time to search and a time to give up, a time to keep and a time to throw away, a time to tear and a time to mend, a time to be silent and a time to speak, a time to love and a time to hate, a time for war and a time for peace.*

PERFORMANCE - EFFECTIVENESS RATIO:

2 KINGS 19:32-36. *"Therefore this is what the LORD says concerning the king of Assyria: "He will not enter this city or shoot an arrow here. He will not come before it with shield or build a siege ramp against it. By the way that he came he will return; he will not enter this city, declares the LORD. I will defend this city and save it, for my sake and for the sake of David my servant."* **That night the angel of the LORD went out and put to death a hundred and eighty-five thousand men in the Assyrian camp. When the people got up the next morning-there were all the dead bodies!** *So Sennacherib king of Assyria broke camp and withdrew. He returned to Nineveh and stayed there.*

JOSH 6:2-5. *Then the LORD said to Joshua, "See, I have delivered Jericho into your hands, along with its king and its fighting men. March around the city once with all the armed men. Do this for six days. Have seven priests carry trumpets of rams' horns in front of the ark.* **On the seventh day, march around the city seven times, with the priests blowing the trumpets. When you hear them sound a long blast on the trumpets, have all the people give a loud shout; then the wall of the city will collapse** *and the people will go up, every man straight in."*

2 KINGS 7:3-7. *And there were four leprous men at the entering in of the gate: and they said one to another, Why sit we here until we die? If we say, We will enter into the city, then the famine is in the city, and we shall die there: and if we sit still here, we die also. Now therefore come, and let us fall unto the host of the Syrians: if they save us alive, we shall live; and if they kill us, we shall but die. And they rose up in the twilight, to go unto the camp of the Syrians: and when they were come to the uttermost part of the camp of Syria, behold, there was no man there.* **For the Lord had made the host of the Syrians to hear a noise of chariots, and a noise of horses, even the noise of a great host: and they said one to another, Lo, the king of Israel hath hired against us the kings of the Hittites, and the kings of the Egyptians, to come upon us. Wherefore they arose and fled in the twilight, and left their tents, and their horses, and their asses, even the camp as it was, and fled for their life.** *KJV*

JUDG 7:2-8. *The LORD said to Gideon,* **"You have too many men for me to deliver Midian into their hands. In order that Israel may not boast against me that her own strength has saved her,** *announce now to the people, 'Anyone who trembles with fear may turn back and leave Mount Gilead.'" So twenty-two thousand men left, while ten thousand remained. But the LORD said to Gideon, "There are still too many men. Take them down to the water, and I will sift them for you there. If I say, 'This one shall go with you,' he shall go; but if I say, 'This one shall not go with you,' he shall not go." So Gideon took the men down to the water. There the LORD told him, "Separate those who lap the water with their tongues like a dog from those who kneel down to drink." Three hundred men lapped with their hands to their mouths. All the rest got down on their knees to drink. The LORD said to Gideon,* **"With the three hundred men that lapped I will save you and give the Midianites into your hands.** *Let all the other men go, each to his own place." So Gideon sent the rest of the Israelites* to their tents but kept the three hundred, who took over the provisions and trumpets of the others.

JUDG 7:15-23. *When Gideon heard the dream and its interpretation, he worshiped God. He returned to the camp of Israel and called out, "Get up! The LORD has given the Midianite camp into your hands." Dividing the three hundred men into three companies, he placed trumpets and empty jars in the hands of all of them, with torches inside. "Watch me," he told them. "Follow my lead. When I get to the edge of the camp, do exactly as I do. When I and all who are with me blow our trumpets, then from all around the camp blow yours and shout, 'For the LORD and for Gideon.'" Gideon and the hundred men with him reached the edge of the camp at the beginning of the middle watch, just after they had changed the guard. They blew their trumpets and broke the jars that were in their hands. The three companies blew the trumpets and smashed the jars. Grasping the torches in their left hands and holding in their right hands the trumpets they were to blow, they shouted, "A sword for the LORD and for Gideon!"* **While each man held his position around the camp, all the Midianites ran, crying out as they fled. When the three hundred trumpets sounded, the LORD caused the men throughout the camp to turn on each other with their swords.** *The army fled to Beth Shittah toward Zererah as far as the border of Abel Meholah near Tabbath.*

PERFORMANCE - KILLERS:

In moments, of what looks like there's a victory, our focus might get distorted by our self-centerism, justifying why we can take something that rightfully doesn't belong to us.

LUKE 9:25. **What good is it for a man to gain the whole world, and yet lose or forfeit his very self?**

JOSH 6:18-19. **But keep away from the devoted things, so that you will not bring about your own destruction by taking any of them.** *Otherwise you will make the camp of Israel liable to destruction and bring trouble on it. All the silver and gold and the articles of bronze and iron are sacred to the LORD and must go into his treasury."*

PERFORMANCE - MOTIVATORS:

ISAIAH 57:10. **You were wearied by all your ways, but you would not say, 'It is hopeless.'** *You found renewal of your strength, and so you did not faint.*

1 THESS 5:14. *And we urge you, brothers, warn those who are idle,* **encourage the timid, help the weak, be patient with everyone.**

2 THESS 2:16-17. *May our Lord Jesus Christ himself and God our Father, who loved us and* **by his grace gave us eternal encouragement and good hope, encourage your hearts and strengthen you in every good deed and word.**

HEB 3:13. **But encourage one another daily,** *as long as it is called Today, so that none of you may be hardened by sin's deceitfulness.*

1 SAM 30:5-6. *David was greatly distressed because the men were talking of stoning him; each one was bitter in spirit because of his sons and daughters.* **But David found strength in the LORD his God.**

REV 2:7. *He who has an ear, let him hear what the Spirit says to the churches.* **To him who overcomes, I will give the right to eat from the tree of life,** *which is in the paradise of God.*

REV 2:26. **To him who overcomes** *and does my will to the end,* **I will give authority over the nations-**

REV 3:4-6. *Yet you have a few people in Sardis who have not soiled their clothes. They will walk with me, dressed in white, for they are worthy.* **He who overcomes will,** *like them, be dressed in white. I will* **never blot out his name from the book of life,** *but will acknowledge his name before my Father and his angels.*

REV 3:11-13. *I am coming soon. Hold on to what you have, so that no one will take your crown.* **Him who overcomes I will make a pillar in the temple of my God.** *Never again will he leave it.* **I will write on him the name of my God and the name of the city of my God, the new Jerusalem,** *which is coming down out of heaven from my God; and* **I will also write on him my new name.** *He who has an ear, let him hear what the Spirit says to the churches.*

REV 21:7-8. **He who overcomes will inherit all this, and I will be his God and he will be my son.**

PERFORMANCE - SUMMARY:

Our performance will reveal which type of protection we chose, how well we can use it and how effective it was in solving our conflicts. It's not that we might live to see the day our conflict is resolved, it's where our heart was in each of the battles we faced along the way. Our heart should be at peace no matter where we are in resolving our conflicts.

2 COR 11:23-29. *I (Paul) have worked much harder, been in prison more frequently, been flogged more severely, and been exposed to death again and again. Five times I received from the Jews the forty lashes minus one. Three times I was beaten with rods, once I was stoned, three times I was shipwrecked, I spent a night and a day in the open sea, I have been constantly on the move. I have been in danger from rivers, in danger from bandits, in danger from my own countrymen, in danger from Gentiles; in danger in the city, in danger in the country, in danger at sea; and in danger from false brothers. I have labored and toiled and have often gone without sleep; I have known hunger and thirst and*

have often gone without food; I have been cold and naked. Besides everything else, I face daily the pressure of my concern for all the churches.

HEB 11:35-39. *others were tortured, not accepting their deliverance; that they might obtain a better resurrection: and others had trial of mockings and scourgings, yea, moreover of bonds and imprisonment: they were stoned, they were sawn asunder, they were tempted, they were slain with the sword: they went about in sheepskins, in goatskins; being destitute, afflicted, ill-treated (of whom the world was not worthy), wandering in deserts and mountains and caves, and the holes of the earth.* **And these all, having had witness borne to them through their faith, received not the promise,** *ASV*

PHIL 4:11-13. **I am not saying this because I am in need, for I have learned to be content whatever the circumstances.** I know what it is to be in need, and I know what it is to have plenty. **I have learned the secret of being content in any and every situation,** whether well fed or hungry, whether living in plenty or in want. I can do everything through him who gives me strength.

ROM 8:28-29. **And we know that in all things God works for the good of those who love him,** who have been called according to his purpose.

Ground Zero

This is where we get real honest about ourselves. Our weakness as sinners/transgressors is to be easy on ourselves.

Prov 16:25. *There is a way that seems right to a man*, but in the end it leads to death, and not admit our weaknesses.

If this revelation makes sense to us, great.

1 COR 2:12-15. *This is what we speak, not in words taught us by human wisdom but in words taught by the Spirit, expressing spiritual truths in spiritual words.* The man without the Spirit does not accept the things that come from the Spirit of God, for they are foolishness to him, and he cannot understand them, because they are spiritually discerned.

If this revelation doesn't make sense to us and we want it to, then we ask the Holy Spirit to open our hearts and minds to understand it.

LUKE 8:25. *"Where is your faith?"* he asked his disciples.

LUKE 17:5. The apostles said to the Lord, *"Increase our faith!"*

JAMES 1:6. *But let him ask in faith, nothing wavering.* For he that wavereth is like a wave of the sea driven with the wind and tossed. KJV

EPH 3:20. Now unto *him that is able to do exceeding abundantly above all that we ask or think,* according to the power that worketh in us, KJV

MARK 11:22-23. And Jesus answering saith unto them, Have faith in God. For verily I say unto you, That whosoever shall say unto this mountain, Be thou removed, and be thou cast into the sea; and shall not doubt in his heart, *but shall believe that those things which he saith shall come to pass; he shall have whatsoever he saith.* KJV

1 PET 2:1. -*Like newborn babies, crave pure spiritual milk, so that by it you may grow up* in your salvation, now that you have tasted that the Lord is good.

LUKE 12:12. for *the Holy Spirit will teach* you at that time what you should say."

1 COR 2:10-15. but *God has revealed it to us by his Spirit. The Spirit searches all things, even the deep things of God.* For who among men knows the thoughts of a man except the man's spirit within him? In the same way no one knows the thoughts of God except the Spirit of God. We have not received the spirit of the world but the Spirit who is from God, that we may understand what God has freely given us. This is what we speak, not in words taught us by human wisdom

but in words taught by the Spirit, expressing spiritual truths in spiritual words. **The man without the Spirit does not accept the things that come from the Spirit of God, for they are foolishness to him,** *and he cannot understand them, because they are spiritually discerned. The spiritual man makes judgments about all things, but he himself is not subject to any man's judgment:*

1 TIM 4:1. *The Spirit clearly says that* **in later times some will abandon the faith and follow deceiving spirits** *and things taught by demons.*

The two biggest battles we're fighting against is our "old nature" and "principalities in high places." Both are hard to detect. And it's doubly troublesome when our enemies can see us far better than we can see them. Until we have the advantage point, we will use this disadvantage as a faith building accelerator. Christ mentioned in...

JOHN 20:29. *Then Jesus told him, "Because you have seen me, you have believed;* **blessed are those who have not seen and yet have believed."**

Armor of God

We believe the first step in *Maximizing the Armor of God* is dissecting Apostle Paul's Armor of God correlation of spiritual truths to physical armor. This is the first variable in taking the Armor of God to the Nth Degree.

Ephesians 6:10-18

Eph 6:10 Finally, be strong in the Lord and in His mighty power.

DISSECTING: Blunt bottom line, don't mess around. Life's a vapor. Our main focus is creating a relationship with God to the point of being one minded with Him. A one minded relationship with God. Aspiring to harness and having God's Glorious power operating in my life, in an impressive way for me and the world. Unity 101.

1 JOHN 4:20-21. *If anyone says, "I love God," yet hates his brother, he is a liar. For anyone who does not love his brother, whom he has seen, cannot love God, whom he has not seen. And he has given us this command: **Whoever loves God must also love his brother.***

LUKE 9:26-27. ***If anyone is ashamed of me and my words, the Son of Man will be ashamed of him** when he comes in his glory and in the glory of the Father and of the holy angels.*

PROV 21:2. *All a man's ways seem right to him, **but the LORD weighs the heart.***

1 COR 6:17. *But he who unites himself with the Lord is one with him in spirit.*

Eph 6:11 Put on the full Armor of God so that you can take your stand against the devil's schemes.

DISSECTING: If we are going to even begin to make an attempt, at neutralizing the devil's schemes, we must start with and make a stand on - not budge - with the Spiritual Understanding of the Armor of God daily. Taking a stand in the sense of staying footed. Looking forward to the point of being determined to get through it. And perhaps enjoy a victory. Armor of God 101.

PROV 4:25-27. *Let your eyes look straight ahead, **fix your gaze directly before you**. Make level paths for your feet and take only ways that are firm. Do not swerve to the right or the left; keep your foot from evil.*

JAMES 1:6-8. ***But let him ask in faith, nothing wavering.** For he that wavereth is like a wave of the sea driven with the wind and tossed. For let not that man think that he shall receive any thing of the Lord. A double minded man is unstable in all his ways. KJV*

Eph 6:12 For our struggle is not against flesh and blood, but against the rulers, against the authorities, against the powers of this dark world and against the spiritual forces of evil in the heavenly realms.

DISSECTING: Paul makes a very clear statement that our struggles/battles are all against spiritual enemies, even though they look and feel as though their all physical. Remember, this is the Paul that was hammering, tarring up Christendom something fierce. Paul has a Christ encounter, makes a 180 and then doubles his efforts in establishing Christendom. Spiritual Warfare 101.

EPH 4:14-15. ***That we henceforth be no more children, tossed to and fro, and carried about with every wind of doctrine, by the sleight of men, and cunning craftiness, whereby they lie in wait to deceive;** But speaking the truth in love, may grow up into him in all things, which is the head, even Christ: KJV*

1 PET 5:8-9. *Be self-controlled and alert. **Your enemy the devil prowls around like a roaring lion looking for someone to devour.** Resist him, standing firm in the faith, because you know that your brothers throughout the world are undergoing the same kind of sufferings.*

Eph 6:13 Therefore put on the full armor of God, so that when the day of evil comes, you may be able to stand your ground, and after you have done everything, to stand.

DISSECTING: Paul is repeating himself. Hmm. He's convinced this is only way we are going to be able to handle the day of evil, by applying the understanding of the Armor of God. There isn't any microwave versions on getting there. It's hard knoxs. Personal Applications. Period. To do this successfully, we need a good working and understanding track record of accumulated personal applications, that have been tested and proven to work effectively. Armor of God 102.

ACTS 19:15-16. *[One day] the evil spirit answered them, "Jesus I know, and I know about Paul, but who are you?" Then the man who had the evil spirit jumped on them and overpowered them all.* He gave them such a beating that they ran out of the house naked and bleeding.

JAMES 4:7-8. Submit yourselves, then, to God. **Resist the devil, and he will flee from you.**

JAMES 1:6-8. But when he asks, he must believe and not doubt, because **he who doubts is like a wave of the sea, blown and tossed by the wind.** That man should not think he will receive anything from the Lord; he is a double-minded man, unstable in all he does.

HEB 6:12. We do not want you to become lazy, but to **imitate those who through faith and patience inherit what has been promised.**

Eph 6:14a Stand firm then, with the belt of truth buckled around your waist,

DISSECTING: No one can refute truth. It's undeniable. It's Creditable. It builds strong foundations. Trustworthy relationships. If we build one truth upon another, one truth at a time, the foundation gets more trustworthy. If we build one lie upon another, one lie at a time, the rock foundation becomes a sand foundation. No one can trust a lie, not even the liar. When push comes to shove, the lie will leave us to ourselves, to defend our self. The truth will always stand beside us to defend us. Push comes to shove; the truth will still be faithful to us, even after all our friends have left us. Usually when one lie is used to cover up another lie, the person who has lied is embarrassed they were caught in the lie. The embracement is like one's boxers falling down to their ankles, unplanned in a public area. Wearing and depending on the truth as a belt bucket around our waist is much like that. Truth 101.

1 COR 2:14-15. The man without the Spirit does not accept the things that come from the Spirit of God, for they are foolishness to him, and he cannot understand them, because they are spiritually discerned. **The spiritual man makes judgments about all things, but he himself is not subject to any man's judgment:**

PROV 16:13. **Kings** take pleasure in honest lips; they **value a man who speaks the truth.**

PSALMS 43:3. **Send forth your light and your truth, let them guide me**; let them bring me to your holy mountain, to the place where you dwell.

JOHN 8:32. Then **you will know the truth, and the truth will set you free.**"

PROV 28:26. He who trusts in himself is a fool, but **he who talks in wisdom is kept safe.**

PSALMS 86:11. **Teach me your way, O LORD, and I will walk in your truth**; given me an undivided heart, that I may fear your name.

1 JOHN 3:18-20. Dear children, **let us not love with words or tongue but with actions and in truth. This then is how we know that we belong to the truth**, and how we set our hearts at rest in his presence whenever our hearts condemn us. For God is greater than our hearts, and he knows everything.

JOHN 16:13-14. But when he, the **Spirit of truth**, comes, he **will guide you into all truth.** He will not speak on his own; he will speak only what he hears, and he will tell you what is yet to come.

Eph 6:14b with the breastplate of righteousness in place,

DISSECTING: The breastplate protects the vital organs -primarily the heart. Where our treasure is, so is our heart. Our treasure, being God's Word is protected by the breastplate of righteousness. Righteousness is a by product of sowing seeds in harmony with God's Word. What will be sown ends up being reaped. Sow righteousness reap righteousness, reaping good things - one primarily being, eternal abundant life. Where as, without this protection, sowing seeds of dis-harmony with God's Word, reaps the by product of wickedness. Wickedness leaves me venerable to reaping wounds (death) to my treasure - my heart - the Word of God, I treasured. This is Sowing Seed 101. Seed sown on rocky soil, just doesn't get enough root to handle the attacks of environmental stress. In this case, spiritual attacks from the enemy. Righteousness 101.

PROV 10:2. Ill-gotten treasures are of no value, but **righteousness delivers from death.**

PROV 11:4-6. Wealth is worthless in the day of wrath, but righteousness delivers from death. **The righteousness of the blameless makes a straight way for them,** *but the wicked are brought down by their own wickedness. The righteousness of the upright delivers them, but the unfaithful are trapped by evil desires.*

PROV 13:6. **Righteousness guards the man of integrity**, *but wickedness overthrows the sinner.*

PROV 16:8. **Better a little with righteousness** *than much gain with injustice.*

PROV 21:21-22. **He who pursues righteousness and love finds life, prosperity and honor.** *A wise man attacks the city of the mighty and pulls down the stronghold in which they trust.*

PROV 25:5. **remove the wicked from the king's presence, and his throne will be established through righteousness.**

MATT 13:20-21. *The one who received the seed that fell on rocky places is the man who hears the word and at once receives it with joy. But since he has no root, he lasts only a short time.* **When trouble or persecution comes because of the word, he quickly falls away.**

Eph 6:15 and with your feet fitted with the readiness that comes from the gospel of peace.

DISSECTING: Feet are associated with traveling. Going places. When we go places we usually interact with people. People have opinions, paradigms about life and styles of communication, some more aggressive than others. Having the knowledge, understanding and the wisdom on how to use the gospel of peace in different interacting moments, increases our odds in saving the lost, let alone our own lives. Gospel of Peace 101.

PROV 3:17-18. *Her ways are pleasant ways, and all her paths are peace.* **She is a tree of life to those who embrace her;** *those who lay hold of her will be blessed.*

PROV 12:20. *There is deceit in the hearts of those who plot evil, but* **joy for those who promote peace.**

PROV 14:30. **A heart at peace gives life to the body,** *but envy rots the bones.*

PROV 16:7. **When a man's ways are pleasing to the LORD, he makes even his enemies live at peace with him.**

JAMES 3:18. **Peacemakers who sow in peace raise a harvest of righteousness.**

MATT 5:9. **Blessed are the peacemakers, for they will be called sons of God.**

Eph 6:16 In addition to all this, take up the shield of faith, with which you can extinguish all the flaming arrows of the evil one.

DISSECTING: A shield is a pre-made portable piece of armor that can be handled with our hands in various positions, to protect us from the path of flying projectiles. Faith, in the form of a shield, implies that the faith is solid enough to protect us from the path of flying projectiles. Our goal is to get our faith so strong, so solid to the point it can defend us at any given moment, on auto pilot. Faith that addresses the predictable attacks that death makes. Example: 80% of the time death uses same tactics and 20% different. The shield of faith takes care of the 80% and the 20% is taken care of by the sword of the spirit. Faith 101.

MATT 4:1-11. *Then Jesus was led by the Spirit into the desert to be tempted by the devil. After fasting forty days and forty nights, he was hungry. The tempter came to him and said, **"If you are the Son of God, tell these stones to become bread." Jesus answered, "It is written: 'Man does not live on bread alone, but on every word that comes from the mouth of God.'"** Then the devil took him to the holy city and had him stand on the highest point of the temple. **"If you are the Son of God,"** he said, **"throw yourself down. For it is written: "'He will command his angels concerning you, and they will lift you up in their hands, so that you will not strike your foot against a stone.'"** Jesus answered him, **"It is also written: 'Do not put the Lord your God to the test.'"** Again, the devil took him to a very high mountain and showed him all the kingdoms of the world and their splendor. **"All this I will give you,"** he said, **"if you will bow down and worship me." Jesus said to him, "Away from me, Satan! For it is written: 'Worship the Lord your God, and serve him only.'"** Then the devil left him, and angels came and attended him.*

Eph 6:17a Take the helmet of salvation

DISSECTING: The helmet protects the head which stores our minds. In our minds, we have a lot of thoughts moving back and forth. Some note worthy. Some chaotic. When we harness our thoughts, we can accomplish some of the most awesome things. To live spiritually or do spiritual battle we need to upgrade our thought process. We do this by taking captive every thought and subjecting to the Word of God. If it matches – own it. If not, we take dominion over it. The helmet of salvation implies we need to take captive every thought and subject it to God's Word, to the point it is on auto pilot. Work it until it becomes an auto pilot thought management system. Salvation 102.

GAL 5:16-18. *So I say,* **live by the Spirit, and you will not gratify the desires of the sinful nature.** *For the sinful nature desires what is contrary to the Spirit, and the Spirit what is contrary to the sinful nature. They are in conflict with each other, so that you do not do what you want.*

ROM 8:5-8. *Those who live according to the sinful nature have their minds set on what that nature desires;* **but those who live in accordance with the Spirit have their minds set on what the Spirit desires.** *The mind of sinful man is death,* **but the mind controlled by the Spirit is life and peace;** *the sinful mind is hostile to God. It does not submit to God's law, nor can it do so. Those controlled by the sinful nature cannot please God.*

REV 1:5-6. *and from Jesus Christ, who is the faithful witness, the firstborn from the dead, and the ruler of the kings of the earth.* **To him who loves us and has freed us from our sins by his blood,**

COL 1:20. **and through him to reconcile to himself all things, whether things on earth or things in heaven, by making peace through his blood,** *shed on the cross.*

EPH 1:7-8. *In him* **we have redemption through his blood**, *the forgiveness of sins, in accordance with the riches of God's grace*

ROM 5:9-11. *Since we have now been justified by his blood, how much more shall we be saved from God's wrath through him! For if, when we were God's enemies,* **we were reconciled to him through the death of his Son, how much more, having been reconciled, shall we be saved through his life!**

ROM 3:22-25. **This righteousness from God comes through faith in Jesus Christ to all who believe.** *There is no difference, for all have sinned and fall short of the glory of God, and are justified freely by his grace through the redemption that came by Christ Jesus. God presented him as a sacrifice of atonement, through faith in his blood. He did this to demonstrate his justice, because in his forbearance he had left the sins committed beforehand unpunished-*

Eph 6:17b and the sword of the Spirit, which is the word of God.

DISSECTING: This is the manual application of applying the Word of God to our specific challenge. We all have our personal walk with God that no one else can share in. It's called having our story about applying God's Word in our lives. Aka "our testimony." Sword of the Spirit 101.

HEB 4:12-13. **For the word of God is living and active. Sharper than any double-edged sword, it penetrates even to dividing soul and spirit, joints and marrow; it judges the thoughts and attitudes of the heart.**

COL 1:25-27. *I have become its servant by the commission God gave me to present to you **the word of God in its fullness**- the mystery that has been kept hidden for ages and generations, but is now disclosed to the saints.*

PROV 30:5. ***"Every word of God is flawless; he is a shield to those who take refuge in him.***

Eph 6:18a And Pray in the Spirit on all occasions with all kinds of prayers and requests.

DISSECTING: Aka Tongues. Encrypted words, coming from our spirits/mouths, that only the Holy Spirit can translate. When the enemy knows our business, we forfeit our advantage point. It's like giving the enemy all of our weapons. All occasions, means all occasions. All kinds of prayers and requests, means the sky is the limit. Plus, God gives us exceedingly abundantly above whatever we ask or think. Lock that all in with, Christ saying we'll would do greater things than He did. Covering the Bases 101.

ROM 8:26-27. *In the same way, the Spirit helps us in our weakness. **We do not know what we ought to pray for, but the Spirit himself intercedes for us with groans that words cannot express. And he who searches our hearts knows the mind of the Spirit,** because the Spirit intercedes for the saints in accordance with God's will.*

Eph 6:18b With this in mind, be alert and always keep on praying for all the saints.

DISSECTING: It's always been a team of people working together for a common goal. Not one person. In this case, protection from an enemy who loves attacking us blind sided. To offset this disadvantage, we sow the seeds of praying for our comrades, fellow warriors: that no matter what state they're in, God would make them strong in His Word; to the point they'll overcome the enemy in their day of battle - blindsided or not. Spiritual Team Buddies 101.

JOHN 17:13-26. *"I am coming to you now, but I say these things while I am still in the world, so that they may have the full measure of my joy within them. I have given them your word and the world has hated them, for they are not of the world any more than I am of the world. **My prayer is not that you take them out of the world but that you protect them from the evil one.** They are not of the world, even as I am not of it. Sanctify them by the truth; your word is truth. As* you sent me into the world, I have sent them into the world. For them I sanctify myself, that they too may be truly sanctified. "My prayer is not for them alone. **I pray also for those who will believe in me through their message, that all of them may be one,** Father, just as you are in me and I am in you. May they also be in us so that the world may believe that you have sent me. I have given them the glory that you gave me, that they may be one as we are one: I in them and you in me. **May they be brought to complete unity to let the world know that you sent me** and have loved them even as you have loved me. "Father, I want those you have given me to be with me where I am, and to see my glory, the glory you have given me because you loved me before the creation of the world. "Righteous Father, though the world does not know you, I know you, and they know that you have sent me. I have made you known to them, and will continue to make you known in order that the love you have for me may be in them and that I myself may be in them."

EPH 4:11-13. It was he who gave some to be apostles, some to be prophets, some to be evangelists, and some to be pastors and teachers, to prepare God's people for works of service, **so that the body of Christ may be built up until we all reach unity in the faith and in the knowledge of the Son of God and become mature, attaining to the whole measure of the fullness of Christ.**

ROM 15:5-6. the God who gives endurance and encouragement give you **a spirit of unity among yourselves as you follow Christ Jesus, with one heart and mouth you may glorify the God and Father of our Lord Jesus Christ.**

PSALMS 133:1. **How good and pleasant it is when brothers live together in unity!**

Blood and Word

Now the body is not made up of one part but of many. If the foot should say, "Because I am not a hand, I do not belong to the body," it would not for that reason cease to be part of the body. And if the ear should say, "Because I am not an eye, I do not belong to the body," it would not for that reason cease to be part of the body. If the whole body were an eye, where would the sense of hearing be? If the whole body were an ear, where would the sense of smell be? But in fact **God has arranged the parts in the body, every one of them, just as he wanted them to be.** *If they were all one part, where would the body be? As it is, there are many parts, but one body.* 1 COR 12:14-20.

This section is intended to give us working examples that will help us focus on taking captive the thoughts that are in our minds, which are contrary to the Word of God. In Revelations it tells us, we over come Death by Christ's Blood. REV 12:11. The Jews were told to put the Passover lamb's blood on the door post so that death would pass them by. EXO 12:13. In the first part of our example, we apply the blood on a body member or item associated with the body. Second, we give scripture references to that body member. For the body members that didn't have any scripture references we used characteristic keywords associated with that body member or item. These are references we found and are listing them here for your convenience. We use the message around the keywords to flesh out the important aspects of each body member or item. God could of made our bodies anyway He wanted to. But in His infinite wisdom, He reasoned to choose these body members we currently have. In our opinion, we believe all the body members, flesh out functions of His character. Thirdly, to help flesh this out more, we listed each of the body members or items attributes. Fourth, we combined the above reference information to draw some observations associated with each function of the body or an item.

Why? Easy, we base this on scripture references. For a reference to the word "bones" we get , PROV 14:30. *a heart at peace gives life to the body, but envy rots the bones.* This statement is indicating that if a person is envious long enough, their bones are going to rot. Hmm. Yah. There's others in scripture, like PROV 17:22. *a merry heart doeth good like a medicine: but a broken spirit drieth the bones.* KJV Here, a broken spirit dries the bones - brittle bones. Plus there are many more which we have listed with each of the body members or items. We took this information and applied it to all the body members or items. When the observation was leaning towards the negative we called it "without it" and when leaning towards the positive, we called it "with it". *Without It* and *With It* categories are in association to if we are applying God's Word in and to our lives or not. If we are, this increases the odds that the body member or item is operating better than if we wasn't applying God's Word. The above are references to negative observations. In the same verses we have some positive observations. They were in the first part of both verses above, PROV 14:30. *a heart at peace gives life to the body.* Hmm. Yah. And PROV 17:22. *a merry heart doeth good like a medicine.*

For some of us, this might be enough to get us on our way to taking captive the thoughts that are contrary to God's Word. But for the rest of us, we'll need to build our artesian wells of God's Word from scratch. Here are some examples to get started with:

No weapon forged against me will prevail ISA 54:17. *Applied this way...* No envy forged against me will prevail in my life.

Step farther...
No <u>envy</u> forged against my (family/congregation/community/business/ government/nation) will prevail against us/them.

<u>Anyone</u> in Christ is a new creation. 2 COR 5:17-18. *Applied this way...* I am a new creation in Christ.

Step farther...
<u>My</u> (family/congregation/community/business/government/nation) are new creations in Christ.

<u>Those</u> who bless Israel will be blessed. GEN 12:3. *Applied this way...* Bless Israel with what you need a breakthrough in. Our example is, <u>We</u> say, as much as envy would like to destroy Israel, *envy will never* enter in their hearts, from this day forth, through out all their generations, forever more.

An over kill? Christ says we'll do greater than Him. So let's start doing it. - Now, <u>we</u> will receive this same blessing, *envy will never* enter in our hearts, from this day forth, through out all our generations, forever more.

Step farther...
<u>We</u> say, as much as envy would like to destroy Israel's (families/ congregations/communities/businesses/government/nation), *it will never* enter in their hearts, from this day forth, through out all their generations, forever more. Now, <u>we</u> will receive this same blessing for our (families/ congregations/communities/businesses/governments/ nations), envy will never enter in our hearts, from this day forth, through out all our generations, forever more.

The prayer of a <u>righteous man</u> is powerful and effective. JAMES 5:16. *Applied this way...* I'm not righteous, My righteousness as filthy rags to God ISAIAH 64:6. but Christ within me, is. Having the faith in believing He died for us, He is God in the flesh and lives within us, all is counted as righteousness. So based on this mind frame, <u>our</u> prayers are powerful and effective.

Step farther...
<u>Our</u> loved ones prayers are powerful and effective.

He who has a bountiful eye will be blessed. Prov 22:9. *Applied this way...* For our example of a bountiful eye, We visualize our break through. We visual our selves living without envy in our lives.

Step farther...
We visualize our (family/congregation/community/business/ government/nation) living without no envy in their lives.

What a man thinketh so is he. Ouch. PROV 23:7. *Applied this way...* We are what we think. We think we can or someday we can live without envy in our lives, with Christ's help.

Step farther...
We can say unto our hearts and minds, yield to thinking only those thoughts that bring life to me and my loved ones, in Jesus Christ Name.

The tongue speaks life or death. PROV 18:21. *Applied this way...* Our tongue will only speak life in my life.

Step farther...
Our (family's/congregation's/community's/business's/government's/ nation's) tongue will only speak life into their lives.

Once we get familiar with this approach, we should go through this loop/cycle until it becomes auto pilot for us.

Now the pain, thoughts and challenges still may come and we will have to deal with them accordingly...pain pills, doctors, etc... But instead of thinking or saying the thoughts or words contrary to the Word of God, we say... the Blood of Jesus Christ... and then the applicable Word of God.

We should never feel guilty, if we never get a particular breakthrough in this phase of life. We wouldn't be the first and we're in good company. HEB 11:4-39. Then the sobering thought, JAMES 1:2-4. God is interested in building our perseverance, to prepare us for future events. Plus, a good word to keep in mind is ISAIAH 49:10... *He who has compassion on them will guide them and lead them beside springs of water.* The only people who have compassion on those who are hurting, are the people who have gone through the pain themselves. Their personal perseverance in the pain becomes a healing and encouraging testimony to those, who are going through the same challenge. Like Christ, He suffered the most, so His compassion on us has more healing and encouragement then anyone else's "word" or opinion about our challenge that is set before us.

The Blood and Word of Jesus Christ is Maximum Protection any human can obtain. Jesus Christ never changes. HEB 13:8. By the Blood of the Lamb and the Word, we overcame the devil. REV 12:11. and the blood of Jesus, His Son, purifies us from all sin. 1 JOHN 1:7b.

The components of our Creator, tangible and intangible, created us in His Image and Likeness, each of these characteristics of God are fleshed out in Jesus Christ. Each member fleshed out in a physical manifestation, finger, eye, etc. So for each body part to maximize its potential, it must be set free from its captivity. This is done by putting / speaking the blood and word on each body part or item. Once this is released, the body part can function at its maximum potential. The minimum for the body should be as like it was in the garden before sin/self-centrism. The maximum should be better than in the garden before sin/self-centrism because now we have Christ and the Holy Spirit.

ROM 8:18-19. *I consider that our present sufferings are not worth comparing with the glory that will be revealed in us. The creation waits in eager expectation for the sons of God to be revealed.*

Once we're on the road to conquering our own thoughts, then we can take this a step further, by including our loved ones; spouses as couples, families, friends, neighbors, communities, nations, fellowships, etc,. MATT 7:3-5. *"Why do you look at the speck of sawdust in your brother's eye and pay no attention to the plank in your own eye? How can you say to your brother, 'Let me take the speck out of your eye,' when all the time there is a plank in your own eye? You hypocrite, first take the plank out of your own eye, and then you will see clearly to remove the speck from your brother's eye.*

Blood of Jesus Christ on my:

BONES so that the Word of God can be a Strong Foundation in my life.

REFERENCES:

JOB 4:14. *fear and trembling seized me and made all my bones shake.*

JOB 21:23-25. *One man dies in full vigor, completely secure and at ease, his body well nourished, his bones rich with marrow.* Another man dies in bitterness of soul, never having enjoyed anything good.

PSALMS 38:3. Because of your wrath there is no health in my body; *my bones have no soundness because of my sin.*

PROV 3:7-8. Do not be wise in your own eyes; *fear the LORD and shun evil. This will bring health to your body and nourishment to your bones.*

PROV 14:30. A heart at peace gives life to the body, *but envy rots the bones.*

PROV 15:30. A cheerful look brings joy to the heart, and *good news gives health to the bones.* PROV 16:24. *Pleasant words are a honeycomb, sweet to the soul and healing to the bones.*

PROV 17:22. A cheerful heart is good medicine, *but a crushed spirit dries up the bones.*

EZEK 37:1-14. The hand of the LORD was upon me, and he brought me out by the Spirit of the LORD and set me in the middle of a valley; it was full of bones. He led me back and forth among them, and I saw a great many bones on the floor of the valley, bones that were very dry. He asked me, "Son of man, can these bones live?" I said, "O Sovereign LORD, you alone know." *Then he said to me, "Prophesy to these bones and say to them, 'Dry bones, hear the word of the LORD! Note: God is no respecter of persons (s) We have the same option to prophesy to our body members or items. Another words, speak or repeat or proclaim or come in agreement with what God's Word says to contrary words or thoughts.* This is what the Sovereign LORD says to these bones: I will make breath enter you, and you will come to life. I will attach tendons to you and make flesh come upon you and cover you with skin; I will put breath in you, and you will come to life. Then you will know that I am the LORD.'" So I prophesied as I was commanded. And as I was prophesying, there was a noise, a rattling sound, and the bones came together, bone to bone. I looked, and tendons and flesh appeared on them and skin covered them, but there was no breath in them. Then he said to me, "Prophesy to the breath; prophesy, son of man, and say to it, 'This is what the Sovereign LORD says: Come from the four winds, O breath, and breathe into these slain, that they may live.' "So I prophesied as he commanded me, and breath entered them; they came to life and stood up on their feet-a vast army. Then he said to me: "Son of man, these bones are the whole house of Israel. They say, 'Our bones are dried up and our hope is gone; we are cut off.' Therefore prophesy and say to them: 'This is what the Sovereign LORD says: O my people, I am going to open your graves and bring you up from them; I will bring you back to the land of Israel. Then you, my people, will know that I am the LORD, when I open your graves and bring you up from them. I will put my Spirit in you and you will live, and I will settle you in your own land. Then you will know that I the LORD have spoken, and I have done it, declares the LORD.'"

JOB 10:10-12. **Did you not pour me out like milk and curdle me like cheese, clothe me with skin and flesh and knit me together with bones and sinews?** You gave me life and showed me kindness, and in your providence watched over my spirit.

PSALMS 89:14. **Righteousness and justice are the foundation of your throne;** love and faithfulness go before you.

ISAIAH 28:16. So this is what **the Sovereign LORD says: "See, I lay a stone in Zion, a tested stone, a precious cornerstone for a sure foundation;** the one who trusts will never be dismayed.

1 TIM 6:17-19. Command them to do good, to be rich in good deeds, and to be generous and willing to share. **In this way they will lay up treasure for themselves as a firm foundation for the coming age,** so that they may take hold of the life that is truly life.

MATT 7:24-27. **"Therefore everyone who hears these words of mine and puts them into practice is like a wise man who built his house on the rock.** The rain came down, the streams rose, and the winds blew and beat against that house; yet it did not fall, because it had its foundation on the rock. But everyone who hears these words of mine and does not put them into practice is like a foolish man who built his house on sand. The rain came down, the streams rose, and the winds blew and beat against that house, and it fell with a great crash."

PHYSICAL ATTRIBUTE ADVANTAGES OF THE BONES: Structure. Core building blocks to allow maximization of amenities.

WITHOUT IT: My backup resources are like sand houses.

WITH IT: I value building my life on a strong foundation. I realize the strength of my foundation is as strong as the amount of the Word of God within me.

FOR COUPLE/GROUP:

Blood of Jesus Christ on our BONES so that the Word of God can be a Strong Foundation in our relationship/s.

Blood of Jesus Christ on my:

SOLES OF MY FEET so that the Word of God can Protect me From my Past and Walk me Through the Future Fires in my life.

REFERENCES:

JOB 13:2-27. *For you write down bitter things against me and make me inherit the sins of my youth. You fasten my feet in shackles;* **you keep close watch on all my paths by putting marks on the soles of my feet.**

MAL 4:3. **Then you will trample down the wicked; they will be ashes under the soles of your feet** *on the day when I do these things,"* says the LORD Almighty.

DEUT 28:33-35. *A people that you do not know will eat what your land and labor produce, and you will have nothing but cruel oppression all your days. The sights you see will drive you mad.* **The LORD will afflict your knees and legs with painful boils that cannot be cured, spreading from the soles of your feet to the top of your head.**

DEUT 11:24-25. **Every place whereon the soles of your feet shall tread shall be yours:** *from the wilderness and Lebanon, from the river, the river Euphrates, even unto the uttermost sea shall your coast be. There shall no man be able to stand before you: for the LORD your God shall lay the fear of you and the dread of you upon all the land that ye shall tread upon, as he hath said unto you. KJV*

ISAIAH 60:14. *The sons also of them that afflicted thee shall come bending unto thee;* **and all they that despised thee shall bow themselves down at the soles of thy feet;** *and they shall call thee, The city of the LORD, The Zion of the Holy One of Israel. KJV*

PHYSICAL ATTRIBUTE ADVANTAGES OF THE SOLES OF MY FEET: Proof of existence and attempts to interact with other entities.

WITHOUT IT: I find myself trapped by previous bad decisions I sowed earlier in my life.

WITH IT: I can successfully conquer areas in my life regardless of the odds against me.

FOR COUPLE/GROUP:

Blood of Jesus Christ on the SOLES OF OUR FEET so that the Word of God can Protect us From our Past/s and Walk us Through the Future Fires in our relationship/s.

Blood of Jesus Christ on my:

FEET so that the Word of God can Stand Firm in my life.

REFERENCES:

PSALMS 37:30-31. *The mouth of the righteous man utters wisdom, and his tongue speaks what is just.* **The law of his God is in his heart; his feet do not slip.**

DEUT 11:24-25. **Every place where you set your foot will be yours:** *Your territory will extend from the desert to Lebanon and from the Euphrates River to the western sea. No man will be able to stand against you. The LORD your God, as he promised you, will put the terror and fear of you on the whole land, wherever you go.*

DEUT 28:64-66. **Among those nations you will find no repose, no resting place for the sole of your foot.** *There the LORD will give you an anxious mind, eyes weary with longing, and a despairing heart.*

PSALMS 121:3. **He will not let your foot slip** — *he who watches over you will not slumber;*

PROV 1:15-19. **my son, do not go along with them, do not set foot on their paths; for their feet rush into sin,** *they are swift to shed blood. How useless to spread a net in full view of all the birds! These men lie in wait for their own blood; they waylay only themselves! Such is the end of all who go after ill-gotten gain; it takes away the lives of those who get it.*

PROV 4:27. *Do not swerve to the right or the left;* **keep your foot** *from evil.*

PHYSICAL ATTRIBUTE ADVANTAGES OF THE FEET: Better balancing, quicker mobility and greater work loads.

WITHOUT IT: I always find myself on the losing side of the key "tug of war" events in my life. Feel uncomfortable in taking sides. My footing is like standing on quick sand.

WITH IT: Allows me to obtain better footing. Better footing allows me to work less in persevering.

FOR COUPLE/GROUP:

Blood of Jesus Christ on our FEET so that the Word of God can Stand Firm in our relationship/s.

Blood of Jesus Christ on my:

JOINTS so that the Word of God can be Leveraged in my life.

REFERENCES:

HEB 4:12-13. *For the word of God is living and active. Sharper than any double-edged sword, it penetrates even to dividing soul and spirit, joints and marrow; it judges the thoughts and attitudes of the heart.*

HEB 11:33-35. *who through faith conquered kingdoms, administered justice, and gained what was promised; who shut the mouths of lions, quenched the fury of the flames, and escaped the edge of the sword; **whose weakness was turned to strength; and who became powerful in battle and routed foreign armies.***

2 COR 12:9-10. *But he said to me, "My grace is sufficient for you, for my power is made perfect in weakness." Therefore I will boast all the more gladly about my weaknesses, so that Christ's power may rest on me. That is why, for Christ's sake, I delight in weaknesses, in insults, in hardships, in persecutions, in difficulties. For when I am weak, then I am strong.*

PHYSICAL ATTRIBUTE ADVANTAGES OF THE JOINTS: Leverage, extra strength and support to handle more weight.

WITHOUT IT: Not much difference between my accomplishments and the worlds.

WITH IT: My weakest weakness is stronger than those who try to over throw me with various types of intimidations

FOR COUPLE/GROUP:

Blood of Jesus Christ on our JOINTS so that the Word of God can be Leveraged in our relationship/s.

Blood of Jesus Christ on my:

RIGHT BIG TOE so that the Word of God will Keep Balanced in my life.

REFERENCES:

PROV 16:11. **Honest scales and balances are from the LORD;** *all the weights in the bag are of his making.*

PROV 11:1. *The LORD abhors dishonest scales, but* **accurate weights are his delight.**

PHYSICAL ATTRIBUTE ADVANTAGES OF THE RIGHT BIG TOE: Leads the way. Makes sacrificial attempts at securing footing for the foot.

WITHOUT IT: My center of gravity is off center. My judgment is in favor of my weakness

WITH IT: Unbiased in all matters of life. Even towards myself. The truth is embraced over favoring my weaknesses

FOR COUPLE/GROUP:

Blood of Jesus Christ on our RIGHT BIG TOES so that the Word of God will Keep Balanced in our relationship/s.

Blood of Jesus Christ on my:

TOES so that the Word of God can Maximize Micro Balancing and Pivoting in my life.

REFERENCES:

DAN 2:41-43. **Just as you saw that the feet and toes were partly of baked clay and partly of iron, so this will be a divided kingdom;** *yet it will have some of the strength of iron in it, even as you saw iron mixed with clay. As the toes were partly iron and partly clay, so this kingdom will be partly strong and partly brittle. And just as you saw the iron mixed with baked clay,* **so the people will be a mixture and will not remain united, any more than iron mixes with clay.**

PHYSICAL ATTRIBUTE ADVANTAGES OF TOE: Balance Assistors. Allows micro adjusting to maximize balancing and pivoting options.

WITHOUT IT: I avoid comforting others.

WITH IT: I address with confidence the deeper issues of life.

FOR COUPLE/GROUP:
Blood of Jesus Christ on our TOES so that the Word of God can Maximize Micro Balancing and Pivoting in our relationship/s.

Blood of Jesus Christ on my:
LEGS so that the Word of God can Walk in and Through the Kingdom of God in my life.

REFERENCES:
PSALMS 1:1. *Blessed is the man who does not walk in the counsel of the wicked or stand in the way of sinners or sit in the seat of mockers.*

PSALMS 86:11. Teach me your way, O LORD, and I will walk in your truth; give me an undivided heart, that I may fear your name.

PSALMS 89:15. Blessed are those who have learned to acclaim you, who walk in the light of your presence, O LORD.

PSALMS 138:7. Though I walk in the midst of trouble, you preserve my life; you stretch out your hand against the anger of my foes, with your right hand you save me.

PROV 2:12-15. Wisdom will save you from the ways of wicked men, from men whose words are perverse, who leave the straight paths to walk in dark ways, who delight in doing wrong and rejoice in the perverseness of evil, whose paths are crooked and who are devious in their ways.

1 JOHN 1:7. But if we walk in the light, as he is in the light, we have fellowship with one another, and the blood of Jesus, his Son, purifies us from all sin.

COL 3:7-10. You used to walk in these ways, in the life you once lived. But now you must rid yourselves of all such things as these: anger, rage, malice, slander, and filthy language from your lips. Do not lie to each other, since you have taken off your old self with its practices and have put on the new self, which is being renewed in knowledge in the image of its Creator.

JOHN 8:12. When Jesus spoke again to the people, he said, "I am the light of the world. Whoever follows me will never walk in darkness, but will have the light of life."

ZECH 3:7. "This is what the LORD Almighty says: 'If you will walk in my ways and keep my requirements, then you will govern my house and have charge of my courts, and I will give you a place among these standing here.

PHYSICAL ATTRIBUTE ADVANTAGES OF THE LEGS: Mobility. Travel. Move work loads. Lifting greater work loads. Networking Leverage/Knees, Interact/Soles, Work Loads/Feet, Balancing/Toes and Accelerators/Thighs.

WITHOUT IT: Avoid Networking outside my local areas of life, work, etc.

WITH IT: I value the bigger picture of life. Leadership Roles are enjoyable.

FOR COUPLE/GROUP:
Blood of Jesus Christ on our LEGS so that the Word of God can Walk in and Through the Kingdom of God in our relationship/s.

Blood of Jesus Christ on my:
RIGHT KNEE so that the Word of God will Submit to the Father in my life.

REFERENCES:

ISAIAH 45:23. *By myself I have sworn, my mouth has uttered in all integrity a word that will not be revoked:* **Before me every knee will bow; by me every tongue will swear.**

EZEK 21:7. *And when they ask you, 'Why are you groaning?' you shall say, 'Because of the news that is coming. Every heart will melt and every hand go limp; **every spirit will become faint and every knee become as weak as water.'** It is coming! It will surely take place, declares the Sovereign LORD."*

ROMANS 14:11-12. **It is written: "'As surely as I live,' says the Lord, 'every knee will bow before me;** every tongue will confess to God.'"* So then, each of us will give an account of himself to God.*

PHIL 2:10-13. **that at the name of Jesus every knee should bow, in heaven and on earth and under the earth,** *and every tongue confess that Jesus Christ is Lord, to the glory of God the Father. Therefore, my dear friends, as you have always obeyed-not only in my presence, but now much more in my* *absence-continue to work out your salvation with fear and trembling, for it is God who works in you to will and to act according to his good purpose.*

PHYSICAL ATTRIBUTE ADVANTAGES OF THE RIGHT KNEE: A different advantage point/perspective. Increases local visual field.

WITHOUT IT: I am rebellious against any hierarchy.

WITH IT: I can willing submit to God's good purpose for my life.

FOR COUPLE/GROUP:
Blood of Jesus Christ on our RIGHT KNEES so that the Word of God will Submit to the Father in our relationship/s.

Blood of Jesus Christ on my:
KNEES so that the Word of God will Run Ahead in my life.

REFERENCES:

PSALMS 20:7-9. *Some trust in chariots and some in horses, but **we trust in the name of the LORD our God.** They are brought to their knees and fall, but **we rise up and stand firm.** O LORD, save the king! Answer us when we call!*

JOB 4:4. *Your words have supported those who stumbled; **you have strengthened faltering knees.***

PSALMS 109:24-25. ***My knees give way from fasting;** my body is thin and gaunt. I am an object of scorn to my accusers; when they see me, they shake their heads.*

HEB 12:12-13. ***Therefore, strengthen your feeble arms and weak knees.** "Make level paths for your feet," so that the lame may not be disabled, but rather healed.*

PHYSICAL ATTRIBUTE ADVANTAGES OF THE KNEES: Provides variable speed mobility option for the body.

WITHOUT IT: I avoid wanting to work with groups of people.

WITH IT: I'm prepared to react to multiple case scenarios.

FOR COUPLE/GROUP:
Blood of Jesus Christ on our KNEES so that the Word of God will Run Ahead in our relationship/s.

Blood of Jesus Christ on my:

RIGHT THIGH so that the Word of God will Wrestle with God for a New Name in my life.

REFERENCES:

GEN 32:24-32. *So Jacob was left alone, and **a man wrestled with him till daybreak.** When the man saw that he could not overpower him, he touched the socket of Jacob's hip so that his hip was wrenched as he wrestled with the man. **Then the man said, "Let me go, for it is daybreak." But Jacob replied, "I will not let you go unless you bless me." The man asked him, "What is your name?" "Jacob," he answered. Then the man said, "Your name will no longer be Jacob, but Israel, because you have struggled with God and with men and have overcome."** Jacob said, "Please tell me your name." But he replied, "Why do you ask my name?" Then he blessed him there. So Jacob called the place Peniel, saying, "It is because I saw God face to face, and yet my life was spared." The sun rose above him as he passed Peniel, and he was limping because of his hip. Therefore to this day the Israelites do not eat the tendon attached to the socket of the hip, because the socket of Jacob's hip was touched near the tendon.*

REV 19:16. *On his robe and **on his thigh he has this name written: KING OF KINGS AND LORD OF LORDS.***

REV 2:17. *He who has an ear, let him hear what the Spirit says to the churches. **To him who overcomes,** I will give some of the hidden manna. **I will also give him a white stone with a new name written on it, known only to him who receives it.***

EXO 29:22. *"Take from this ram the fat, the fat tail, the fat around the inner parts, the covering of the liver, **both kidneys with the fat on them, and the right thigh.***

LEV 7:32-34. *__You are to give the right thigh of your fellowship offerings to the priest as a contribution.__ The son of Aaron who offers the blood and the fat of the fellowship offering shall have the right thigh as his share. From the fellowship offerings of the Israelites, I have taken the breast that is waved and the thigh that is presented and have given them to Aaron the priest and his sons as their regular share from the Israelites.'"*

PHYSICAL ATTRIBUTE ADVANTAGES OF THE RIGHT THIGH:
Provides acceleration to mobility options.

WITHOUT IT: My family name is mock, ridiculed and defamed. No end to my earthly struggles.

WITH IT: I grab a hold of my destiny with dignity, strength and no fear.

FOR COUPLE/GROUP:

Blood of Jesus Christ on our RIGHT THIGHS so that the Word of God will Wrestle with God for a New Name in our relationship/s.

Blood of Jesus Christ on my:

THIGHS so that the Word of God can Wrestle for My Destiny in my life.

REFERENCES:

JOB 40:17. *His tail sways like a cedar;* ***the sinews of his thighs are lose-knit.***

DAN 2:32-33. *The head of the statue was made of pure gold, its chest and arms of silver,* ***its belly and thighs of bronze,***

GEN 24:1-4. *He said to the chief servant in his household, the one in charge of all that he had,* ***"Put your hand under my thigh. I want you to swear by the LORD, the God of heaven and the God of earth,*** *that you will not get a wife for my son from the daughters of the Canaanites, among whom I am living, but will go to my country and my own relatives and get a wife for my son Isaac."*

GEN 47:28-30. *When the time drew near for Israel to die, he called for his son Joseph and said to him,* ***"If I have found favor in your eyes, put your hand under my thigh and promise that you will show me kindness and faithfulness.*** *Do not bury me in Egypt,*

NUM 5:21. *here the priest is to put the woman under this curse of the oath —* ***"may the LORD cause your people to curse and denounce you when he causes your thigh to waste away and your abdomen to swell.***

REV 19:16. *On his robe and* ***on his thigh he has this name written: KING OF KINGS AND LORD OF LORDS.***

GEN 32:25-32. ***When the man saw that he could not overpower him, he touched the socket of Jacob's hip so that his hip was wrenched as he wrestled with the man.*** *Then the man said, "Let me go, for it is daybreak." But Jacob replied, "I will not let you go unless you bless me." The man asked him, "What is your name?" "Jacob," he answered. Then the man said, "Your name will no longer be Jacob, but Israel, because you have struggled with God and with men and have overcome." Jacob said, "Please tell me your name." But he replied, "Why do you ask my name?" Then he blessed him there. So Jacob called the place Peniel, saying, "It is because I saw God face to face, and yet my life was spared." The sun rose above him as he passed Peniel, and he was limping because of his hip. Therefore to this day the Israelites do not eat the tendon attached to the socket of the hip, because the socket of Jacob's hip was touched near the tendon.*

PHYSICAL ATTRIBUTE ADVANTAGES OF THE THIGHS: Spin Torque accelerators. Stamina. Endurance.

WITHOUT IT: I avoid building my legacy. I accept my mediocre life as the best it gets.

WITH IT: I embrace what God has destined me to be in Him. I'm fluid in allowing the Holy Spirit transform me.

FOR COUPLE/GROUP:
Blood of Jesus Christ on our THIGHS so that the Word of God can Wrestle for our Destinies in our relationship/s.

Blood of Jesus Christ on my:
BUTTOCKS so that the Word of God can have Dominion in my life.

REFERENCES:

JOB 25:2. "***Dominion and awe belong to God;*** *he establishes order in the heights of heaven.*

JOB 38:33. *Do you know the laws of the heavens?* ***Can you set up [God's] dominion over the earth?***

PSALMS 22:28. ***for dominion belongs to the LORD and he rules over the nations.***

PSALMS 145:13. ***Your kingdom is an everlasting kingdom, and your dominion endures through all generations.*** *The LORD is faithful to all his promises and loving toward all he has made.*

DAN 4:3. *How great are his signs, how mighty his wonders!* ***His kingdom is an eternal kingdom; his dominion endures from generation to generation.***

DAN 6:26. "*I issue a decree that in every part of my kingdom people must fear and reverence the God of Daniel.* "*For he is the living God and he endures forever;* ***his kingdom will not be destroyed, his dominion will never end.***

DAN 7:14. ***He was given authority, glory and sovereign power;*** *all peoples, nations and men of every language worshiped him.* ***His dominion is an everlasting dominion that will not pass away, and his kingdom is one that will never be destroyed.***

1 COR 15:23-28. *Then the end will come, when he hands over the kingdom to* ***God the Father after he has destroyed all dominion, authority and power. For he must reign until he has put all his enemies under his feet. The last enemy to be destroyed is death.*** *For he* "*has put everything under his feet.*" *Now when*

it says that "everything" has been put under him, it is clear that this does not include God himself, who put everything under Christ. When he has done this, then the Son himself will be made subject to him who put everything under him, so that God may be all in all.

EPH 1:20-23. **far above all rule and authority, power and dominion, and every title that can be given, not only in the present age but also in the one to come.** And God placed all things under his feet and appointed him to be head over everything for the church, which is his body, the fullness of him who fills everything in every way.

COL 1:13-14. **For he has rescued us from the dominion of darkness and brought us into the kingdom of the Son he loves,** in whom we have   redemption, the forgiveness of sins.

ISAIAH 16:5. **In love a throne will be established; in faithfulness a man will sit on it** — one from the house of David — one who in judging seeks justice and speeds the cause of righteousness.

PSALMS 132:12. **if your sons keep my covenant and the statutes I teach them, then their sons will sit on your throne for ever and ever."**

PSALMS 97:2. Clouds and thick darkness surround him; **righteousness and justice are the foundation of his throne.**

REV 7:10. **And they cried out in a loud voice: "Salvation belongs to our God, who sits on the throne, and to the Lamb."**

REV 3:21-22. To him who overcomes, **I will give the right to sit with me on my throne, just as I overcame and sat down with my Father on his throne.**

HEB 4:16. **Let us then approach the throne of grace with confidence,** so that we may receive mercy and find grace to help us in our time of need.

MATT 22:44. **"'The Lord said to my Lord: "Sit at my right hand until I put your enemies under your feet."** '

PHYSICAL ATTRIBUTE ADVANTAGES OF THE BUTTOCKS: Rest. Authority. Body protection when going backwards.

WITHOUT IT: I'm restless. Paranoia gets the best of me. I feel like a slave.

WITH IT: I'm driven to lead by example, emanating the fruits of faithfulness and compassion.

FOR COUPLE/GROUP:

Blood of Jesus Christ on our BUTTOCKS so that the Word of God can have Dominion in our relationship/s.

Blood of Jesus Christ on my:

SIDE so that the Word of God can Develop Relationships that Glorify God in my life.

REFERENCES:

JOB 29:4. *Oh, for the days when I was in my prime,* **when God's intimate friendship blessed my house,**

1 SAM 20:42. *Jonathan said to David,* **"Go in peace, for we have sworn friendship with each other in the name of the LORD, saying, 'The LORD is witness between you and me, and between your descendants and my descendants forever.'"** *Then David left, and Jonathan went back to the town.*

PROV 12:26. **A righteous man is cautious in friendship,** *but the way of the wicked leads them astray.*

JAMES 4:4. *You adulterous people, don't you know that friendship with the world is hatred toward God?* **Anyone who chooses to be a friend of the world becomes an enemy of God.**

PHYSICAL ATTRIBUTE ADVANTAGES OF THE SIDE: Perimeters that allow me to enjoy the moment/width but reminds me to stay focused on the future that/which lies ahead.

WITHOUT IT: I find myself only accepting the artificial side of people. Alliances are only skin deep.

WITH IT: A healthy strong network of supporters fill my life. After a hard days work I can rest peacefully with my loved ones in my home.

FOR COUPLE/GROUP:

Blood of Jesus Christ on our SIDES so that the Word of God can Develop Relationships that Glorify God in our relationship/s.

Blood of Jesus Christ on my:

BACK so that the Word of God can Lighten the Burdens in my life.

REFERENCES:

MATT 11:28-30. **"Come to me, all you who are weary and burdened, and I will give you rest.** *Take my yoke upon you and learn from me, for I am gentle and* humble in heart, and you will find rest for your souls. For my yoke is easy and my burden is light."

PSALMS 68:19. *Praise be to the Lord, **to God our Savior, who daily bears our burdens.***

PSALMS 38:6-8. *I am bowed down and brought very low; all day long I go about mourning. **My back is filled with searing pain;** there is no health in my body. I am feeble and utterly crushed; I groan in anguish of heart.*

PHYSICAL ATTRIBUTE ADVANTAGES OF THE BACK: Manipulates an environment that provides a "state" of rest.

WITHOUT IT: It's easier for me to fulfill other people's dreams than my own.

WITH IT: A healthy network of support will gel together to create a legacy for proceeding generations.

FOR COUPLE/GROUP:

Blood of Jesus Christ on our BACKS so that the Word of God can Lighten the Burdens in our relationship/s.

Blood of Jesus Christ on my:

CHEST so that the Word of God can be Received as a Little Child in my life.

REFERENCES:

JERE 31:19. *After I strayed, I repented; after I came to understand, **I beat my breast. I was ashamed and humiliated because I bore the disgrace of my youth.'***

GEN 49:25-26. *because of your father's God, who helps you, because of the Almighty, who blesses you with blessings of the heavens above, **blessings of the deep that lies below, blessings of the breast and womb.** Your father's blessings are greater than the blessings of the ancient mountains, than the bounty of the age-old hills. Let all these rest on the head of Joseph, on the brow of the prince among his brothers.*

LUKE 18:17. *I tell you the truth, **anyone who will not receive the kingdom of God like a little child will never enter it."***

LUKE 9:46-48. *Jesus, knowing their thoughts, took a little child and had him stand beside him. Then he said to them, "**Whoever welcomes this little child in*** *my name welcomes me; and whoever welcomes me welcomes the one who sent me. For he who is least among you all-he is the greatest."*

LUKE 10:19-20. *I have given you authority to trample on snakes and scorpions and to overcome all the power of the enemy; nothing will harm you. However, do not rejoice that the spirits submit to you, but rejoice that your names are written in heaven."*

PHYSICAL ATTRIBUTE ADVANTAGES OF THE CHEST: Provides protection for vital amenities.

WITHOUT IT: I tend to be mischievous. I avoid being accountable for my actions.

WITH IT: I am captivated at living life through the eyes of a toddler.

FOR COUPLE/GROUP:
Blood of Jesus Christ on our CHESTS so that the Word of God can be Received as a Little Child in our relationship/s.

Blood of Jesus Christ on my:
BREAST so that the Word of God can be Nourishment in my life.

REFERENCES:

JOB 24:9. *The fatherless child is snatched from the breast; the infant of the poor is seized for a debt.*

PSALMS 22:9. *Yet you brought me out of the womb; you made me trust in you even at my mother's breast.*

ISAIAH 49:15. *"Can a mother forget the baby at her breast and have no compassion on the child she has borne? Though she may forget, I will not forget you!*

JER 31:19. *After I strayed, I repented; after I came to understand, I beat my breast. I was ashamed and humiliated because I bore the disgrace of my youth.'*

JOEL 2:16. *Gather the people, consecrate the assembly; bring together the elders, gather the children, those nursing at the breast. Let the bridegroom leave his room and the bride her chamber.*

PHYSICAL ATTRIBUTE ADVANTAGES OF THE BREAST: Provides Natural Immunities to Protect Against Diseases, Nutrition for Body Development and Beauty.

WITHOUT IT: I tend to give into oppressors. Anemic. I feel unattractive.

WITH IT: I embrace healthy, resourceful and radiant relationships.

FOR COUPLE/GROUP:
Blood of Jesus Christ on our BREASTS so that the Word of God can be Nourishment in our relationship/s.

Blood of Jesus Christ on my:
RIGHT SHOULDER so that the Word of God can have Velocity in my life.

REFERENCES:

EXO 28:12, 21. *and fasten them on the shoulder pieces of the ephod as memorial stones for the sons of Israel.* **Aaron is to bear the names on his shoulders as a memorial before the LORD.** *There are to be twelve stones, one for each of the names of the sons of Israel, each engraved like a seal with the name of one of the twelve tribes.*

ISAIAH 22:22-24. **I will place on his shoulder the key to the house of David; what he opens no one can shut, and what he shuts no one can open.** *I will drive him like a peg into a firm place; he will be a seat of honor for the house of his father. All the glory of his family will hang on him: its offspring and offshoots — all its lesser vessels, from the bowls to all the jars.*

ZEPH 3:9. **"Then will I purify the lips of the peoples, that all of them may call on the name of the LORD and serve him shoulder to shoulder.**

PHYSICAL ATTRIBUTE ADVANTAGES OF THE RIGHT SHOULDER: Accelerates impact of work loads.

WITHOUT IT: No immediate family unity. No enriching greater family accomplishments.

WITH IT: My family and community is blessed under my hierarchy.

FOR COUPLE/GROUP:
Blood of Jesus Christ on our RIGHT SHOULDERS so that the Word of God can have Velocity in our relationship/s.

Blood of Jesus Christ on my:

SHOULDERS so that the Word of God can Accomplish the Required Task in my life.

REFERENCES:

GEN 21:14. *Early the next morning Abraham took some food and a skin of water and gave them to Hagar.* **He set them on her shoulders and then sent her off with the boy.** *She went on her way and wandered in the desert of Beersheba.*

EXO 12:34. **So the people took their dough before the yeast was added, and carried it on their shoulders in kneading troughs wrapped in clothing.**

EXO 28:12-13. *and fasten them on the shoulder pieces of the ephod as memorial stones for the sons of Israel.* **Aaron is to bear the names on his shoulders as a memorial before the LORD.**

NUM 7:9. *But Moses did not give any to the Kohathites,* **because they were to carry on their shoulders the holy things,** *for which they were responsible.*

DEUT 33:12. *About Benjamin he said: "Let the beloved of the LORD rest secure in him, for he shields him all day long,* **and the one the LORD loves rests between his shoulders."**

NEH 3:4-5. *Meremoth son of Uriah, the son of Hakkoz, repaired the next section. Next to him Meshullam son of Berekiah, the son of Meshezabel, made repairs, and next to him Zadok son of Baana also made repairs.* **The next section was repaired by the men of Tekoa, but their nobles would not put their shoulders to the work under their supervisors.**

PSALMS 81:6. **He says, "I removed the burden from their shoulders;** *their hands were set free from the basket.*

ISAIAH 9:6-7. **For to us a child is born, to us a son is given, and the government will be on his shoulders.** *And he will be called Wonderful Counselor, Mighty God, Everlasting Father, Prince of Peace. Of the increase of his government and peace there will be no end. He will reign on David's throne and over his kingdom, establishing and upholding it with justice and righteousness from that time on and forever. The zeal of the LORD Almighty will accomplish this.*

ISAIAH 10:27 27. **In that day their burden will be lifted from your shoulders,** *their yoke from your neck; the yoke will be broken because you have grown so fat.*

ISAIAH 14:25. *I will crush the Assyrian in my land; on my mountains I will trample him down.* **His yoke will be taken from my people, and his burden removed from their shoulders."**

ISAIAH 49:22. *This is what the Sovereign LORD says: "See, I will beckon to the Gentiles, I will lift up my banner to the peoples;* **they will bring your sons in their arms and carry your daughters on their shoulders.**

MATT 23:1-4. *Then Jesus said to the crowds and to his disciples: "The teachers of the law and the Pharisees sit in Moses' seat. So you must obey them and do everything they tell you. But do not do what they do, for they do not practice what they preach.* **They tie up heavy loads and put them on men's shoulders,** *but they themselves are not willing to lift a finger to move them.*

LUKE 15:3-7. *Then Jesus told them this parable: "Suppose one of you has a hundred sheep and loses one of them. Does he not leave the ninety-nine in the open country and* **go after the lost sheep until he finds it? And when he finds it, he joyfully puts it on his shoulders and goes home.** *Then he calls his friends and neighbors together and says, 'Rejoice with me; I have found my lost sheep.'*

PHYSICAL ATTRIBUTE ADVANTAGES OF THE SHOULDERS: Load positioners, resters that assist in accomplishing a task.

WITHOUT IT: I'm a slave to those who are using me for their own desires.

WITH IT: I accept the responsibility of watching and making loved ones burdens lighter.

FOR COUPLE/GROUP:

Blood of Jesus Christ on our SHOULDERS so that the Word of God can Accomplish the Required Tasks in our relationship/s.

Blood of Jesus Christ on my:

ARMS so that the Word of God can be Comforting in my life.

REFERENCES:

MATTHEW 5:4. **Blessed are those who mourn, for they will be comforted.**

ISAIAH 66:13. **As a mother comforts her child, so will I comfort you;** *and you will be comforted over Jerusalem."*

ISAIAH 54:11. **"O afflicted city, lashed by storms and not comforted,** *I will build you with stones of turquoise, your foundations with sapphires.*

PSALMS 86:17. *Give me a sign of your goodness, that my enemies may see it and be put to shame, for you,* **O LORD, have helped me and comforted me.**

PSALMS 119:76-77. *May your unfailing love be my comfort, according to your promise to your servant. Let your compassion come to me that I may live, for your law is my delight.*

PSALMS 23:4. *Even though I walk through the valley of the shadow of death, I will fear no evil, for you are with me; **your rod and your staff, they comfort me.***

JOB 16:5. *But my mouth would encourage you; **comfort from my lips would bring you relief.***

PROV 31:17. *She sets about her work vigorously; **her arms are strong for her tasks.***

ISAIAH 49:22. *This is what the Sovereign LORD says: "See, I will beckon to the Gentiles, I will lift up my banner to the peoples; **they will bring your sons in their arms** and carry your daughters on their shoulders.*

HEB 12:11-12. *No discipline seems pleasant at the time, but painful. Later on, however, it produces a harvest of righteousness and peace for those who have been trained by it. Therefore, **strengthen your feeble arms and weak knees.***

LUKE 15:20. *So he got up and went to his father. "But while he was still a long way off, **his father saw him and was filled with compassion for him;** he ran to his son, threw his arms around him and kissed him.*

MARK 10:14-16. *When Jesus saw this, he was indignant. He said to them, "Let the little children come to me, and do not hinder them, for the kingdom of God belongs to such as these. I tell you the truth, anyone who will not receive the kingdom of God like a little child will never enter it." **And he took the children in his arms, put his hands on them and blessed them.***

PROV 31:20. ***She opens her arms to the poor and extends her hands to the needy.***

ISAIAH 49:10. *They will neither hunger nor thirst, nor will the desert heat or the sun beat upon them. **He who has compassion on them will guide them and lead them beside springs of water.***

PHYSICAL ATTRIBUTE ADVANTAGES OF THE ARMS: Comfort.
Networking Leverage/Elbows, Design/Hands, Positioning/Wrists, Prosperity/Thumbs and Manifests Entities/Fingers.

WITHOUT IT: I can't see the benefits of discipline. It's hard giving people an extended hug. I tend to avoid having compassion on people.

WITH IT: I'm quick to minister to people's needs based on nobody helping me out when I was going through my challenges.

FOR COUPLE/GROUP:
Blood of Jesus Christ on our ARMS so that the Word of God can be Comforting in our relationship/s.

Blood of Jesus Christ on my:
RIGHT ELBOW so that the Word of God can be Leveraged Exponentially in my life.

REFERENCES:

PSALMS 81:6. **He says, "I removed the burden from their shoulders; their hands were set free from the basket.**

ECCL 3:9-14. *What does the worker gain from his toil? I have seen the   burden God has laid on men. He has made everything beautiful in its time. He has also set eternity in the hearts of men; yet they cannot fathom what God has done from beginning to end. I know that there is nothing better for men than to be happy and do good while they live.* **That everyone may eat and drink, and find satisfaction in all his toil-this is the gift of God.**

MATT 11:29-30. **Take my yoke upon you** *and learn from me, for I am gentle and humble in heart,* **and you will find rest for your souls.** *For my yoke is easy and my burden is light."*

PROV 21:22. **A wise man attacks the city of the mighty and pulls down the stronghold in which they trust.**

EPH 6:10-11. **Finally, be strong in the Lord and in his mighty power.**

PHYSICAL ATTRIBUTE ADVANTAGES OF THE RIGHT ELBOW:
Leverage greater than normal.

WITHOUT IT: I'm not happy with my career choices.

WITH IT: Deep revelations are revealed on the mysteries that have my curiosity when I seek God.

FOR COUPLE/GROUP:
Blood of Jesus Christ on our RIGHT ELBOWS so that the Word of God can be Leveraged Exponentially in our relationship/s.

Blood of Jesus Christ on my:
ELBOWS so that the Word of God can Labor in my life.

53

REFERENCES:

PSALM 127:1. *Unless the LORD builds the house, its builders labor in vain.* *Unless the LORD watches over the city, the watchmen stand guard in vain.*

PSALMS 128:1-2. *Blessed are all who fear the LORD, who walk in his ways.* *You will eat the fruit of your labor; blessings and prosperity will be yours.*

PSALMS 107:11-16. *for they had rebelled against the words of God and despised the counsel of the Most High.* *So he subjected them to bitter labor; they stumbled, and there was no one to help.* *Then they cried to the LORD in their trouble, and he saved them from their distress. He brought them out of darkness and the deepest gloom and broke away their chains.* *Let them give thanks to the LORD for his unfailing love and his wonderful deeds for men, for he breaks down gates of bronze and cuts through bars of iron.*

PROV 12:24. *Diligent hands will rule,* but laziness ends in slave labor.

PHYSICAL ATTRIBUTE ADVANTAGES OF THE RIGHT ELBOW:
Accelerates replacement cycles.

WITHOUT IT: My labor bears no fruit. I will have limited choices on how I can enjoy myself in my free time.

WITH IT: I maximize my mobility at my leisure with my immediate family.

FOR COUPLE/GROUP:

Blood of Jesus Christ on our ELBOWS so that the Word of God can Labor in our relationship/s.

Blood of Jesus Christ on my:

WRIST so that the Word of God can Rightly Position my life.

REFERENCES:

GEN 38:28-30. *As she was giving birth, one of them put out his hand; so the midwife took a scarlet thread and tied it on his wrist and said, "This one came out first." But when he drew back his hand, his brother came out, and she said, "So this is how you have broken out!"* And he was named Perez. Then his brother, who had the scarlet thread on his wrist, came out and he was given the name Zerah.

JUDGE 7:21. *While each man held his position around the camp, all the Midianites ran, crying out as they fled.*

PHYSICAL ATTRIBUTE ADVANTAGES OF THE WRIST: Precision Positioning.

WITHOUT IT: I tend to justify my insensitivity instead of making personal adjustments for others in my life.

WITH IT: I take the time to readjusted reposition my life so that others can connect with me better. I tend to assist others to learn how to assist others.

FOR COUPLE/GROUP:
Blood of Jesus Christ on our WRISTS so that the Word of God can Rightly Position our relationship/s.

Blood of Jesus Christ on my:
HANDS so that the Word of God can create God's Design Purpose in my life.

REFERENCES:

PSALMS 127:1. *A song of ascents. Of Solomon.* **Unless the LORD builds the house, its builders labor in vain.** *Unless the LORD watches over the city, the watchmen stand guard in vain.*

JERE 1:5. **"Before I formed you in the womb I knew you,** *before you were born I set you apart; I appointed you as a prophet to the nations."*

ISAIAH 55:11. *so is my word that goes out from my mouth: It will not return to me empty,* **but will accomplish what I desire and achieve the purpose for which I sent it.**

PSALMS 138:8. *The LORD will fulfill [his purpose] for me; your love,* **O LORD, endures forever — do not abandon the works of your hands.**

PSALMS 28:4. *Repay them for their deeds and for their evil work;* **repay them for what their hands have done** *and bring back upon them what they deserve.*

PHYSICAL ATTRIBUTE ADVANTAGES OF THE HANDS: Manipulate entities for added resources, healing and description analyses.

WITHOUT IT: My hands constantly tare down what God wants to build up in my life.

WITH IT: God protects His accomplishments in my life by dismantling my fears.

FOR COUPLE/GROUP:

Blood of Jesus Christ on our HANDS so that the Word of God can create God's Design Purpose in our relationship/s.

Blood of Jesus Christ on my:

RIGHT THUMB so that the Word of God can Prosper in and for my life.

REFERENCES:

EXO 29:20-21. *Slaughter it, **take some of its blood and put it on** the lobes of the right ears of Aaron and his sons, on **the thumbs of their right hands,** and on the big toes of their right feet. Then sprinkle blood against the altar on all sides.*

LEV 8:24-25. *Moses also brought Aaron's sons forward and **put some of the blood** on the lobes of their right ears, **on the thumbs of their right hands** and on the big toes of their right feet. Then he sprinkled blood against the altar on all sides.*

PROV 11:25. *A generous man will prosper; **he who refreshes others will himself be refreshed.***

JERE 29:11. *For I know the plans I have for you," declares the LORD, **"plans to prosper you and not to harm you, plans to give you hope and a future.***

PHYSICAL ATTRIBUTE ADVANTAGES OF THE RIGHT THUMB:
Accelerates grip cycles.

WITHOUT IT: All of my wants and needs leave me thirsty. Never quenched. Restlessness.

WITH IT: Freedom to be free in being like God. My prosperity quenches my wants and needs.

FOR COUPLE/GROUP:

Blood of Jesus Christ on our RIGHT THUMBS so that the Word of God can Prosper in and for our relationship/s.

Blood of Jesus Christ on my:

THUMBS so that the Word of God can Have Grip in and for my life.

REFERENCES:

ECCL 2:26. *To the man who pleases him, God gives wisdom, knowledge and happiness,* **but to the sinner he gives the task of gathering and storing up wealth to hand it over to the one who pleases God.** *This too is meaningless, a chasing after the wind.*

JUDGE 1:4-7. *When Judah attacked, the LORD gave the Canaanites and Perizzites into their hands and they struck down ten thousand men at Bezek. It was there that they found Adoni-Bezek and fought against him, putting to rout the Canaanites and Perizzites. Adoni-Bezek fled, but they chased him and caught him, and* **cut off his thumbs** *and big toes. Then Adoni-Bezek said, "Seventy kings with their thumbs and big toes cut off have picked up scraps under my table. Now God has paid me back for what I did to them." They brought him to Jerusalem, and he died there.*

PROV 28:13. *He who conceals his sins does not prosper,* **but whoever confesses and renounces them finds mercy.**

PHYSICAL ATTRIBUTE ADVANTAGES OF THE THUMBS: Provides interlocking grip.

WITHOUT IT: I can't get a handle on my challenges.

WITH IT: I'm recognized for my abilities to get results during the most challenging moments.

FOR COUPLE/GROUP:

Blood of Jesus Christ on our THUMBS so that the Word of God can Have Grip in and for our relationship/s.

Blood of Jesus Christ on my:

FINGERS so that the Word of God can Manifest God's Design Purpose in my life.

REFERENCES:

PSALMS 8:3. **When I consider your heavens, the work of your fingers,** *the moon and the stars, which you have set in place,*

PSALMS 144:1. *Praise be to the* **LORD my Rock, who trains** *my hands for war,* **my fingers for battle.**

PROV 6:13-15. *who winks with his eye, signals with his feet and* **motions with his fingers, who plots evil with deceit in his heart** *— he always stirs up* *dissension. Therefore disaster will overtake him in an instant; he will suddenly be destroyed — without remedy.*

PROV 7:3. **Bind them on your fingers;** *write them on the tablet of your heart.*

ISAIAH 2:8. *Their land is full of idols;* **they bow down** *to the work of their hands,* **to what their fingers have made.**

ISAIAH 59:3. *For your hands are stained with blood,* **your fingers with guilt.** *Your lips have spoken lies, and your tongue mutters wicked things.*

DAN 5:5-6. **Suddenly the fingers of a human hand appeared and wrote on the plaster of the wall,** *near the lamp stand in the royal palace. The king watched the hand as it wrote.*

EXO 8:19. *The magicians said to Pharaoh,* **"This is the finger of God."** *But Pharaoh's heart was hard and he would not listen, just as the LORD had said.*

LEV 4:17-19. **He shall dip his finger into the blood and sprinkle it before the LORD seven times in front of the curtain.** *He is to put some of the blood on the horns of the altar that is before the LORD in the Tent of Meeting. The rest of the blood he shall pour out at the base of the altar of burnt offering at the entrance to the Tent of Meeting.*

LUKE 11:20. **But if I drive out demons by the finger of God,** *then the kingdom of God has come to you.*

PHYSICAL ATTRIBUTE ADVANTAGES OF THE FINGERS: Manifests entities for added resources, healing and description analyses.

WITHOUT IT: My selfish fantasies leave me stranded and empty handed.

WITH IT: I have no guilt in establishing the Kingdom of God.

FOR COUPLE/GROUP:
Blood of Jesus Christ on our FINGERS so that the Word of God can Manifest God's Design Purpose in our relationship/s.

Blood of Jesus Christ on my:
NECK so that the Word of God can Connect Thought and Action in my life.

REFERENCES:

GEN 49:8. *"Judah, your brothers will praise you;* **your hand will be on the neck of your enemies;** *your father's sons will bow down to you.*

DEUT 28:48. *therefore in hunger and thirst, in nakedness and dire poverty, you will serve the enemies the LORD sends against you.* **He will put an iron yoke on your neck until he has destroyed you.**

JOB 41:22. **Strength resides in his neck;** *dismay goes before him.*

PROV 3:3. **Let love and faithfulness never leave you; bind them around your neck,** *write them on the tablet of your heart.*

ISAIAH 10:27. **In that day their burden will be lifted from your shoulders, their yoke from your neck;** *the yoke will be broken because you have grown so fat.*

PHYSICAL ATTRIBUTE ADVANTAGES OF THE NECK: Increase vision spectrum. Sphere mobility. Connects thoughts to fulfillment of thoughts.

WITHOUT IT: I lean towards being intimidated by how people talk versus who they are.

WITH IT: Foreigners will put me in charge of their manipulation of entities for added resources, healing and description analyses operations.

FOR COUPLE/GROUP:

Blood of Jesus Christ on our NECKS so that the Word of God can Connect Thoughts and Actions in our relationship/s.

Blood of Jesus Christ on my:

HEAD so that the Word of God can be Meditated on Day and Night in my life.

REFERENCES:

JOSH 1:8-9. *Do not let this Book of the Law depart from your mouth;* **meditate on it day and night,** *so that you may be careful to do everything written in it. Then you will be prosperous and successful. Have I not commanded you? Be strong and courageous. Do not be terrified; do not be discouraged, for the LORD your God will be with you wherever you go."* PSALMS 119:97-99. *Oh, how* **I love your law! I meditate on it all day long.** *Your commands make me wiser than my enemies, for they are ever with me.* **I have more insight than all my teachers, for I meditate on your statutes.**

PROV 10:24. *What the wicked dreads will overtake him;* **what the righteous desire will be granted.**

DEUT 28:12-14. *The LORD will open the heavens, the storehouse of his bounty, to send rain on your land in season and to bless all the work of your hands. You will lend to many nations but will borrow from none.* **The LORD will make you the head, not the tail. If you pay attention to the commands of the LORD your God** *that I give you this day and carefully follow them, you will always be at the top, never at the bottom.*

PHYSICAL ATTRIBUTE ADVANTAGES OF THE HEAD: Leadership skills. Orchestrates body to accomplish desires goals on auto pilot.

WITHOUT IT: My thoughts are over whelmed with fear of being poor and unsuccessful.

WITH IT: I become what good desires I think/focus on. It's the Fuel that ignites encouragement in my times of doubt.

FOR COUPLE/GROUP:
Blood of Jesus Christ on our HEADS so that the Word of God can be Meditated on Day & Night in our relationship/s.

Blood of Jesus Christ on my:
FOREHEAD so that the Word of God can Keep Moving Forward in my life.

REFERENCE:

EZEK 3:7-9. *But the house of Israel is not willing to listen to you because they are not willing to listen to me, for the whole house of Israel is hardened and obstinate.* **But I will make you as unyielding and hardened as they are. I will make your forehead like the hardest stone, harder than flint.** *Do not be afraid of them or terrified by them, though they are a rebellious house."*

PHYSICAL ATTRIBUTE ADVANTAGES OF THE FOREHEAD: Determination, Perseverance. Eyes must look ahead to the future.

WITHOUT IT: I will become afraid and turn away. I will choose a path of lesser resistance. I will become weak. My standard will be stronger than God's standard. God's plans for my life will be put in neutral.

WITH IT: I understand the importance/end results of being able to head butt against destructive principalities.

FOR COUPLE/GROUP:
Blood of Jesus Christ on our FOREHEADS so that the Word of God can Keep Moving Forward in our relationship/s.

Blood of Jesus Christ on my:

RIGHT EAR LOBE so that the Word of God can Manifest the Faith Required in my life.

REFERENCES:

DEUT 15:16-17. *But if your servant says to you, "I do not want to leave you," because he loves you and your family and is well off with you,* **then take an awl and push it through his ear lobe into the door, and he will become your servant for life.** *Do the same for your maidservant.*

LEV 8:22-24. *He then presented the other ram, the ram for the ordination, and Aaron and his sons laid their hands on its head.* **Moses slaughtered the ram and took some of its blood and put it on the lobe of Aaron's right ear,** *on the thumb of his right hand and on the big toe of his right foot. Moses also brought Aaron's sons forward and put some of the blood on the lobes of their right ears, on the thumbs of their right hands and on the big toes of their right feet. Then he sprinkled blood against the altar on all sides.*

LEV 14:14-18. **The priest is to take some of the blood of the guilt offering and put it on the lobe of the right ear of the one to be cleansed,** *on the thumb of his right hand and on the big toe of his right foot. The priest shall then take some of the log of oil, pour it in the palm of his own left hand, dip his right forefinger into the oil in his palm, and with his finger sprinkle some of it before the LORD seven times. The priest is to put some of the oil remaining in his palm on the lobe of the right ear of the one to be cleansed, on the thumb of his right hand and on the big toe of his right foot, on top of the blood of the guilt offering. The rest of the oil in his palm the priest shall put on the head of the one to be cleansed and make atonement for him before the LORD.*

PHYSICAL ATTRIBUTE ADVANTAGES OF THE RIGHT EAR LOBE:
Assists in collection of spoken desires.

WITHOUT IT: My desires take precedent. I tend to manipulate God's desires into conforming to mine. I don't listen to the people I care about.

WITH IT: I clearly hear God's Word. When I hear God's Word it solidifies into applicable form. The invisible becomes visible.

FOR COUPLE/GROUP:
Blood of Jesus Christ on our RIGHT EAR LOBES so that the Word of God can Manifest the Faith Required in our relationship/s.

Blood of Jesus Christ on my:
EARS so that the Word of God can Receive the Faith Required in my life.

REFERENCES:

ISAIAH 6:10. *Make the heart of this people calloused; make their ears dull and close their eyes.* **Otherwise they might see with their eyes, hear with their ears, understand with their hearts, and turn and be healed."**

ROMANS 10:17-18. **Consequently, faith comes from hearing the message, and the message is heard through the word of Christ.** *But I ask: Did they not hear? Of course they did: "Their voice has gone out into all the earth, their words to the ends of the world."*

MATT 13:14. *In them is fulfilled the prophecy of Isaiah:* **"'You will be ever hearing but never understanding;** *you will be ever seeing but never perceiving.*

AMOS 8:11-12. *"The days are coming," declares the Sovereign LORD, "when* **I will send a famine through the land- not a famine of food or a thirst for water, but a famine of hearing the words of the LORD.** *Men will stagger from sea to sea and wander from north to east, searching for the word of the LORD, but they will not find it.*

PHYSICAL ATTRIBUTE ADVANTAGES OF THE EARS: Corridor to Abundant Life. The Gateway to Eternal Life.

WITHOUT IT: My thoughts bounce in opposite directions. I lean to listening to what my worldly thoughts think are right.

WITH IT: I'm perceptive to the opportunities that will have the greatest impact on my life.

FOR COUPLE/GROUP:
Blood of Jesus Christ on our EARS so that the Word of God can Receive the Faith Required in our relationship/s.

Blood of Jesus Christ on my:

NOSE so that the Word of God can be a Sweet Aroma in my life.

REFERENCES:

PROV 30:33. *For as churning the milk produces butter,* **and as twisting the nose produces blood, so stirring up anger produces strife."**

2 COR 2:14-17. **But thanks be to God, who always leads us in triumphal procession in Christ and through us spreads everywhere the fragrance of the knowledge of him. For we are to God the aroma of Christ among those who are being saved and those who are perishing. To the one we are the smell of death; to the other, the fragrance of life.** *And who is equal to such a task? Unlike so many, we do not peddle the word of God for profit. On the contrary, in Christ we speak before God with sincerity, like men sent from God.*

PHYSICAL ATTRIBUTE ADVANTAGES OF THE NOSE: Heightens Specific Conditions of Surrounding Areas.

WITHOUT IT: I'm unaware of the immediate needs needing attention.

WITH IT: I can discern fragile moments/encounters and respond appropriately.

FOR COUPLE/GROUP:

Blood of Jesus Christ on our NOSES so that the Word of God can be a Sweet Aroma in our relationship/s.

Blood of Jesus Christ on my:

SKIN so that the Word of God can Hold Together the Life in my life.

REFERENCES:

EZEK 37:7-8. **I looked, and tendons and flesh appeared on them and skin covered them, but there was no breath in them.**

JOB 7:5. *My body is clothed with worms and scabs,* **my skin is broken and festering.**

COL 1:17-20. *He is before all things, and* **in him all things hold together.** *And he is the head of the body, the church; he is the beginning and the firstborn from among the dead, so that in everything he might have the supremacy. For God* *was pleased to have all his fullness dwell in him, and through him to reconcile to himself all things, whether things on earth or things in heaven, by making peace through his blood, shed on the cross.*

PHYSICAL ATTRIBUTE ADVANTAGES OF THE SKIN: Covering for the body so that the body's parts can have an intimate relationship with one another without outside interference.

WITHOUT IT: No matter who the person is and their intentions are, I can not distinguish the importance of confidentiality.

WITH IT: Proactive in respecting mental, physical and spiritual boundaries.

FOR COUPLE/GROUP:
Blood of Jesus Christ on our SKIN so that the Word of God can Hold Together the Life in our relationship/s.

Blood of Jesus Christ on my:
HAIR so that the Word of God can be Adorned and Anointed in my life.

REFERENCES:

JER 10:3-5. **For the customs of the peoples are worthless;** *they cut a tree out of the forest, and a craftsman shapes it with his chisel. They adorn it with silver and gold; they fasten it with hammer and nails so it will not totter. Like a scarecrow in a melon patch, their idols cannot speak; they must be carried because they cannot walk. Do not fear them; they can do no harm nor can they do any good."*

JER 4:30. *What are you doing, O devastated one?* **Why dress yourself in scarlet and put on jewels of gold?** *Why shade your eyes with paint?* **You adorn yourself in vain.** *Your lovers despise you; they seek your life.*

JOB 40:10. **Then adorn yourself with glory and splendor,** *and clothe yourself in honor and majesty.*

PSALMS 20:6. *Now I know that* **the LORD saves his anointed**; *he answers him from his holy heaven with the saving power of his right hand.*

PSALMS 105:14-15. *He allowed no one to oppress them; for their sake he rebuked kings: "***Do not touch my anointed ones***; do my prophets no harm."*

LUKE 4:18-19. **"The Spirit of the Lord is on me, because he has anointed me** *to preach good news to the poor. He has sent me to proclaim freedom for the* prisoners and recovery of sight for the blind, to release the oppressed, to proclaim the year of the Lord's favor."

1 SAM 16:13. So **Samuel took the horn of oil and anointed him** in the presence of his brothers, and from that day on the Spirit of the LORD came upon David in power. Samuel then went to Ramah.

PHYSICAL ATTRIBUTE ADVANTAGES OF THE HAIR: Celebration Enhancements.

WITHOUT IT: My relationships and work always seems incomplete. I'm insisting on asking for one more detail.

WITH IT: I'm satisfied with what was accomplished with my relationships and work for that day. I can celebrate what was or wasn't accomplished today.

FOR COUPLE/GROUP:

Blood of Jesus Christ on our HAIR so that the Word of God can be Adorned and Annointed in our relationship/s.

Blood of Jesus Christ on my:

MIND so that the Word of God can Create a New Mind in Christ Jesus in my life.

REFERENCES:

PSALMS 26:2-3. Test me, O LORD, and try me, **examine my heart and my mind;** for your love is ever before me, and I walk continually in your truth.

ISAIAH 32:6. **For the fool speaks folly, his mind is busy with evil:** He practices ungodliness and spreads error concerning the LORD; the hungry he leaves empty and from the thirsty he withholds water.

1 THES 4:11-12. **Make it your ambition to lead a quiet life, to mind your own business and to work with your hands,** just as we told you, so that your daily life may win the respect of outsiders and so that you will not be dependent on anybody.

1 COR 14:15-16. So what shall I do? I will pray with my spirit, but I will also pray with my mind; **I will sing with my spirit, but I will also sing with my mind.**

ROMANS 1:28-32. Furthermore, since they did not think it worthwhile to retain the knowledge of God, **he gave them over to a depraved mind, to do what ought not to be done.** They have become filled with every kind of wickedness, evil, greed and depravity. They are full of envy, murder, strife, deceit and malice.

They are gossips, slanderers, God-haters, insolent, arrogant and boastful; they invent ways of doing evil; they disobey their parents; they are senseless, faithless, heartless, ruthless. Although they know God's righteous decree that those who do such things deserve death, they not only continue to do these very things but also approve of those who practice them.

ROMANS 8:6. *The mind of sinful man is death, but the mind controlled by the Spirit is life and peace;*

ROMANS 12:2. *Do not conform any longer to the pattern of this world, but be transformed by the renewing of your mind.* Then you will be able to test and approve what God's will is-his good, pleasing and perfect will.

2 COR 10:5. *We demolish arguments and every pretension that sets itself up against the knowledge of God,* and we take captive every thought to make it obedient to Christ.

PHYSICAL ATTRIBUTE ADVANTAGES OF THE MIND: Prioritizes thoughts and physically manifests them pending limitations.

WITHOUT IT: I'm convinced, my set of priorities are rightly justified by my false paradigms.

WITH IT: I'm determined to press on at aligning and setting my beliefs on a foundation of eternal truths.

FOR COUPLE/GROUP:
Blood of Jesus Christ on our MINDS so that the Word of God can Create a New Mind in Christ Jesus in our relationship/s.

Blood of Jesus Christ on my:
NERVOUS SYSTEM so that the Word of God can be at Peace in my life.

REFERENCES:

PSALMS 4:8. *I will lie down and sleep in peace,* for you alone, O LORD, make me dwell in safety.

PROV 3:17-18. *Her ways are pleasant ways, and all her paths are peace.* She is a tree of life to those who embrace her; those who lay hold of her will be blessed.

PROV 16:7. *When a man's ways are pleasing to the LORD, he makes even his enemies live at peace with him.*

PROV 14:30. *A heart at peace gives life to the body*, but envy rots the bones.

ISAIAH 57:11. *"There is no peace,"* says my God, *"for the wicked."*

MATT 10:13. *If the home is deserving, let your peace rest on it*; if it is not, let your peace return to you.

2 PET 1:2. *Grace and peace be yours in abundance through the knowledge of God and of Jesus our Lord.*

JAMES 3:18. *Peacemakers who sow in peace raise a harvest of righteousness.*

HEB 12:11. No *discipline* seems pleasant at the time, but painful. Later on, however, it *produces a harvest of righteousness and peace for those who have been trained by it.*

PHYSICAL ATTRIBUTE ADVANTAGES OF THE NERVOUS SYSTEM: Peace. Love. Hot and Cold. Rough and Smooth.

WITHOUT IT: I lean towards defending who I am or "think I am" no matter the cost.

WITH IT: With dignity intact, I understand and receive the benefits of applying eternal truths.

FOR COUPLE/GROUP:
Blood of Jesus Christ on our NERVOUS SYSTEMS so that the Word of God can be at Peace in our relationship/s.

Blood of Jesus Christ on my:
RIGHT EYE so that the Word of God can Encourage in my life.

REFERENCES:

PSALMS 94:9. Does he who implanted the ear not hear? *Does he who formed the eye not see?*

PROV 7:2. Keep my commands and you will live; *guard my teachings as the apple of your eye.*

ECCL 1:8. All things are wearisome, more than one can say. *The eye never has enough of seeing,* nor the ear its fill of hearing.

ISAIAH 29:20. The ruthless will vanish, the mockers will disappear, and *all who have an eye for evil will be cut down —*

ZECH 11:17. *"**Woe to the worthless shepherd**, who deserts the flock! **May the sword strike** his arm and his **right eye**! May his arm be completely withered, **his right eye totally blinded!**"*

MATT 6:22-23. *"**The eye is the lamp of the body. If your eyes are good, your whole body will be full of light.** But if your eyes are bad, your whole body will be full of darkness. If then the light within you is darkness, how great is that darkness!*

ROMANS 1:11-12. *I **long to see you so that I may impart to you some spiritual gift to make you strong-** that is, that you and I may be mutually encouraged by each other's faith.*

COL 2:2-4. ***My purpose is that they may be encouraged in heart and united in love,** so that they may have the full riches of complete understanding, in order that they may know the mystery of God, namely, Christ, in whom are hidden all the treasures of wisdom and knowledge. I tell you this so that no one may deceive you by fine-sounding arguments.*

PHYSICAL ATTRIBUTE ADVANTAGES OF THE RIGHT EYE: Depth Perception, quick entity description and quicker reaction times.

WITHOUT IT: I never get to see what I was hoping to see. I tend to believe more in my reality then in my hopes.

WITH IT: I can see how my controlled and out of control circumstances are guiding me to the fulfillment of my desires.

FOR COUPLE/GROUP:
Blood of Jesus Christ on our RIGHT EYES so that the Word of God can Encourage in our relationship/s.

Blood of Jesus Christ on my:
EYES so that the Word of God can Bring into View the Kingdom of God in my life.

REFERENCES:

LUKE 11:33-34. ***Your eye is the lamp of your body. When your eyes are good, your whole body also is full of light.** But when they are bad, your body also is full of darkness.*

LUKE 8:10. *He said, "The knowledge of the secrets of the kingdom of God has been given to you, but to others **I speak in parables, so that, "'though seeing, they may not see;** though hearing, they may not understand.'*

1 COR 4:19-21. **For the kingdom of God is** *not a matter of talk but of* **power.**

JOHN 3:5. *Jesus answered, "I tell you the truth,* **no one can enter the kingdom of God unless he is born of water and the Spirit.**

LUKE 17:21. *nor will people say, 'Here it is,' or 'There it is,'* **because the kingdom of God is within you."**

MARK 1:15. **"The time has come,"** *he said.* **"The kingdom of God is near.** *Repent and believe the good news!"*

PHYSICAL ATTRIBUTE ADVANTAGES OF THE EYES: Accelerates Comprehension.

WITHOUT IT: I hopelessly look for clues that will lead to answers of which will explain the chaos in my life.

WITH IT: I see the invisible answers that lead me through the bridgeless events in my life.

FOR COUPLE/GROUP:
Blood of Jesus Christ on our EYES so that the Word of God can Bring into View the Kingdom of God in our relationship/s.

Blood of Jesus Christ on my:
PITUITARY GLAND so that the Word of God can Nurture my life.

REFERENCES:

PSALMS 1:3. **He is like a tree planted by streams of water, which yields its fruit in season and whose leaf does not wither.** *Whatever he does prospers.*

JER 17:8. **He will be like a tree planted by the water that sends out its roots by the stream.** *It does not fear when heat comes; its leaves are always green. It has no worries in a year of drought* **and never fails to bear fruit."**

JER 1:12. *Then said the LORD unto me, Thou hast well seen: for I will hasten my word to perform it.*

PHYSICAL ATTRIBUTE ADVANTAGES OF THE PITUITARY GLAND:

Produces growth, adrenaline, prolactin hormones and assists the thyroid gland.

WITHOUT IT: I lean towards obtaining growth, health and temperance with an unbalanced life style, even if it costs me my life.

WITH IT: I experience balanced growth, health and temperance.

FOR COUPLE/GROUP:
Blood of Jesus Christ on our PITUITARY GLANDS so that the Word of God can Nurture our relationship/s.

Blood of Jesus Christ on my:
RIGHT NOSTRIL so that the Word of God can be Discerned in my life.

REFERENCES:

PROV 28:11. *A rich man may be wise in his own eyes, but **a poor man who has discernment sees through him.***

PROV 17:10. ***A rebuke impresses a man of discernment** more than a hundred lashes a fool.*

PROV 3:21-24. ***My son, preserve sound judgment and discernment,** do not let them out of your sight; **they will be life for you,** an ornament to grace your neck. Then you will go on your way in safety, and your foot will not stumble; **when you lie down, you will not be afraid;** when you lie down, your sleep will be sweet.*

PSALMS 119:125. *I am your servant; **give me discernment that I may understand your statutes.***

I KINGS 3:11-14. **So God said to him, "Since you have asked for this and not for long life or wealth for yourself, nor have asked for the death of your enemies but for discernment in administering justice,** *I will do what you have asked.* **I will give you a wise and discerning heart,** *so that there will never have been anyone like you, nor will there ever be. Moreover, I will give you what you have not asked for-both riches and honor-so that in your lifetime you will have no equal among kings. And if you walk in my ways and obey my statutes and commands as David your father did, I will give you a long life."*

DUET 32:28-29. *They are a nation without sense, there is no discernment in them. **If only they were wise and would understand this and discern what their end will be!***

COR 12:4,7,10-11. *There are different kinds of gifts, but the same Spirit. **Now to each one the manifestation of the Spirit is given for the common good.** to another miraculous powers, to another prophecy, **to another distinguishing between spirits,** to another speaking in different kinds of tongues, and to still another* the interpretation of tongues. All these are the work of one and the same Spirit, and he gives them to each one, just as he determines.

PHYSICAL ATTRIBUTE ADVANTAGES OF THE RIGHT NOSTRIL: Perception of Conditions.

WITHOUT IT: I don't understand the consequences and ramifications of my decisions. Stuck in decision making rut.

WITH IT: I can clearly decipher unbiasly my and people's intentions.

FOR COUPLE/GROUP:

Blood of Jesus Christ on our RIGHT NOSTRILS so that the Word of God can be Discerned in our relationship/s.

Blood of Jesus Christ on my:

NOSTRILS so that the Word of God can be Sustained in my life.

REFERENCES:

GEN 2:7. **the LORD God formed the man** from the dust of the ground **and breathed into his nostrils the breath of life,** and the man became a living being.

GEN 7:22. **Everything on dry land that had the breath of life in its nostrils died.**

EXO 15:8. **By the blast of your nostrils the waters piled up.** The surging waters stood firm like a wall; the deep waters congealed in the heart of the sea.

NUM 11:19-20. **You will not eat it** for just one day, or two days, or five, ten or twenty days, but for a whole month — **until it comes out of your nostrils** and you loathe it — because you have rejected the LORD, who is among you, and have wailed before him, saying, "Why did we ever leave Egypt?' '"

2 SAM 22:16. The valleys of the sea were exposed and the foundations of the **earth laid bare at the rebuke of the LORD, at the blast of breath from his nostrils.**

JOB 27:3. **as long as I have life within me, the breath of God in my nostrils,**

ISAIAH 2:22. **Stop trusting in man, who has but a breath in his nostrils.** Of what account is he?

AMOS 4:10. "I sent plagues among you as I did to Egypt. I killed your young men with the sword, along with your captured horses. **I filled your nostrils with** the stench of your camps, yet you have not returned to me," *declares the LORD.*

GEN 8:21-22. *The LORD smelled the pleasing aroma and said in his heart: "Never again will I curse the ground because of man, even though every inclination of his heart is evil from childhood.* And never again will I destroy all living creatures, as I have done. "As long as the earth endures, seedtime and harvest, cold and heat, summer and winter, day and night will never cease."

2 COR 2:15-17. *For we are to God the aroma of Christ among those who are being saved and those who are perishing. To the one we are the smell of death; to the other, the fragrance of life. And who is equal to such a task?*

PHYSICAL ATTRIBUTE ADVANTAGES OF THE NOSTRILS: Aroma Value Analyzer.

WITHOUT IT: My general conclusion about my life is "it stinks."

WITH IT: My life style is therapeutic to those I interact with.

FOR COUPLE/GROUP:
Blood of Jesus Christ on our NOSTRILS so that the Word of God can be Sustained in our relationship/s.

Blood of Jesus Christ on my:
LIPS so that the Word of God can Produce Variable Sounds in my life.

REFERENCES:
PSALMS 63:3. *Because your love is better than life, **my lips will glorify you.***

PROV 12:19. ***Truthful lips endure forever,*** *but a lying tongue lasts only a moment.*

PROV 8:7. *My mouth speaks what is true, **for my lips detest wickedness.***

PROV 10:13. ***Wisdom is found on the lips of the discerning,*** *but a rod is for the back of him who lacks judgment.*

PROV 10:21. ***The lips of the righteous nourish many,*** *but fools die for lack of judgment.*

PROV 10:32. ***The lips of the righteous know what is fitting,*** *but the mouth of the wicked only what is perverse.*

PROV 13:2. ***From the fruit of his lips a man enjoys good things,*** *but the unfaithful have a craving for violence.*

PROV 13:3. **He who guards his lips guards his life**, *but he who speaks rashly will come to ruin.*

PROV 15:7. **The lips of the wise spread knowledge;** *not so the hearts of fools.*

PROV 16:13. **Kings take pleasure in honest lips;** *they value a man who speaks the truth.*

PROV 18:7. **A fool's mouth is his undoing, and his lips are a snare to his soul.**

PROV 18:20. **From the fruit of his mouth a man's stomach is filled;** *with the harvest from his lips he is satisfied.*

PROV 24:26. **An honest answer is like a kiss on the lips.**

PROV 26:24. **A malicious man disguises himself with his lips, but in his heart he harbors deceit.**

ISAIAH 29:13. **The Lord says: "These people come near to me with their mouth and honor me with their lips, but their hearts are far from me.** *Their worship of me is made up only of rules taught by men.*

PHYSICAL ATTRIBUTE ADVANTAGES OF THE LIPS: Directional Air Vents to create sounds.

WITHOUT IT: I hear my lips saying things to cover up what I'm really thinking.

WITH IT: I enjoy nourishing people with knowledge, wisdom and honesty.

FOR COUPLE/GROUP:
Blood of Jesus Christ on our LIPS so that the Word of God can Produce Variable Sounds in our relationship/s.

Blood of Jesus Christ on my:
MOUTH so that the Word of God can be Spoken in, Through and Over my life.

REFERENCES:

PROV 10:11. **The mouth of the righteous is a fountain of life**, *but violence overwhelms the mouth of the wicked.*

PSALMS 119:43. **Do not snatch the word of truth from my mouth**, *for I have put my hope in your laws.*

1 PET 4:11. ***If anyone speaks, he should do it as one speaking the very words of God.*** *If anyone serves, he should do it with the strength God provides, so that in all things God may be praised through Jesus Christ. To him be the glory and the power for ever and ever. Amen.*

PROV 14:3. ***A fool's talk brings a rod to his back***, *but the lips of the wise protect them.*

ROMANS 15:5-6. *May the God who gives endurance and encouragement give you* ***a spirit of unity among yourselves as you follow Christ Jesus, so that with one heart and mouth you may glorify the God and Father of our Lord Jesus Christ.***

PHYSICAL ATTRIBUTE ADVANTAGES OF THE MOUTH: Vessel that delivers, assists, accompanies dominion.

WITHOUT IT: Decay erodes everything/everyone associated with my life to the point of death.

WITH IT: Wisely chosen words accomplish more with less physical effort. Doomed relationships are resurrected.

FOR COUPLE/GROUP:

Blood of Jesus Christ on our MOUTHS so that the Word of God can be Spoken in, Through and Over our relationship/s.

Blood of Jesus Christ on my:

TEETH so that the Word of God can Feed on the Goodness in my life.

REFERENCES:

JOB 4:10. ***The lions may roar and growl, yet the teeth of the great lions are broken.***

JOB 29:17. ***I broke the fangs of the wicked and snatched the victims from their teeth.***

PSALMS 3:7. ***Arise, O LORD! Deliver me***, *O my God! Strike all my enemies on the jaw;* ***break the teeth of the wicked.***

DEUT 6:10-12. ***When the LORD your God brings you into the land*** *he swore to your fathers, to Abraham, Isaac and Jacob,* ***to give you*** *— a land with large,* ***flourishing cities you did not build***, *houses filled with all kinds of good things you did not provide, wells you did not dig, and vineyards and olive groves you did not plant —* ***then when you eat and are satisfied, be careful that you do not forget the LORD***, *who brought you out of Egypt, out of the land of slavery.*

EZRA 9:12. **Do not seek a treaty of friendship with them at any time, that you may be strong and eat the good things of the land** and leave it to your children as an everlasting inheritance.'

NUM 31:27. **Divide the spoils between the soldiers who took part in the battle** and the rest of the community.

PHYSICAL ATTRIBUTE ADVANTAGES OF THE TEETH: Dissects and Crushes Entities/Mysteries for the Body to Benefit.

WITHOUT IT: I lean towards dealing with concepts that most people comprehend with common sense.

WITH IT: I'm aggressive about acquiring the knowledge that creates strong foundations.

FOR COUPLE/GROUP:
Blood of Jesus Christ on our TEETH so that the Word of God can Feed on the Goodness in our relationship/s.

Blood of Jesus Christ on my:
WISDOM TOOTH so that the Word of God can Wisely Refine the Word of God in my life.

REFERENCES:

DEUT 4:5-6. **Observe them carefully, for this will show your wisdom and understanding to the nations,** who will hear about all these decrees and say, "**Surely this great nation is a wise and understanding people.**"

PROV 17:24. **A discerning man keeps wisdom in view,** but a fool's eyes wander to the ends of the earth.

PROV 19:11. **A man's wisdom gives him patience;** it is to his glory to overlook an offense.

ECCL 7:12. **Wisdom is a shelter as money is a shelter,** but the advantage of knowledge is this: that wisdom preserves the life of its possessor.

ECCL 7:19. **Wisdom makes one wise man more powerful than ten rulers in a city.**

ECCL 9:18. **Wisdom is better than weapons of war,** but one sinner destroys much good.

JER 9:23-24. This is what the LORD says: **"Let not the wise man boast of his wisdom** or the strong man boast of his strength or the rich man boast of his riches, but let him who boasts boast about this: that he understands and knows *me, that I am the LORD, who exercises kindness, justice and righteousness on earth, for in these I delight," declares the LORD.*

PHYSICAL ATTRIBUTE ADVANTAGES OF THE TEETH: Provides Extra torque on Dissecting and Crushing Entities/Mysteries for the Body to Benefit.

WITHOUT IT: I lean towards numbing /extracting the tools from my life that will assist me in appreciating the deeper simplicities of life.

WITH IT: I understand how to utilize mysteries for the benefit of all systems.

FOR COUPLE/GROUP:
Blood of Jesus Christ on our WISDOM TEETH so that the Word of God can Wisely Refine the Word of God our relationship/s.

Blood of Jesus Christ on my:
TONGUE so that the Word of God can be Speak Life in my life.

REFERENCES:

JOHN 8:54-55. *Jesus replied, "If I glorify myself, my glory means nothing. **My Father**, whom you claim as your God, **is the one who glorifies me.***

PSALMS 5:9. *Not **a word from their mouth can be trusted**; their heart is filled with destruction. Their throat is an open grave; **with their tongue they speak deceit.***

PSALMS 35:28. ***My tongue will speak of your righteousness** and of your praises all day long.*

PSALMS 39:3. *My heart grew hot within me, and **as I meditated, the fire burned; then I spoke with my tongue:***

PROV 18:21. ***The tongue has the power of life and Death**, and those who love it will eat its fruit.*

PROV 15:4. ***The tongue that brings healing is a tree of life**, but a deceitful tongue crushes the spirit.*

PROV 12:19. *Truthful lips endure forever, but **a lying tongue lasts only a moment.***

PROV 12:18. *Reckless words pierce like a sword,* **but the tongue of the wise brings healing.**

PROV 26:28. **A lying tongue hates those it hurts,** *and a flattering mouth works ruin.*

JAMES 1:26. **If anyone considers himself religious and yet does not keep a tight rein on his tongue, he deceives himself and his religion is worthless.**

JAMES 3:4-6. *Likewise the tongue is a small part of the body, but it makes great boasts. Consider what a great forest is set on fire by a small spark.* **The tongue also is a fire**, *a world of evil among the parts of the body. It corrupts the whole person,* **sets the whole course of his life on fire,** *and is itself set on fire by hell.*

JAMES 3:9-12. **With the tongue we praise our Lord and Father, and with it we curse men, who have been made in God's likeness.** *Out of the same mouth come praise and cursing.* **My brothers, this should not be.** *Can both fresh water and salt water flow from the same spring?*

PHYSICAL ATTRIBUTE ADVANTAGES OF THE TONGUE: Nutritional Value Analyzer.

WITHOUT IT: I find myself always saying something no matter if it's good or bad.

WITH IT: People enjoy the fruits and encouragements of my tongue, in present or copy.

FOR COUPLE/GROUP:
Blood of Jesus Christ on our TONGUES so that the Word of God can Speak Life in our relationship/s.

Blood of Jesus Christ on my:
TONSILS so that the Word of God can Guard me in my life.

REFERENCES:

GEN 42:9. *Then he remembered his dreams about them and said to them, "You are spies!* **You have come to see where our land is unprotected."**

JOSH 2:1-3. *Then Joshua son of Nun secretly sent two spies from Shittim. "Go, look over the land," he said, "especially Jericho." So they went and entered the house of a prostitute named Rahab and stayed there. The king of Jericho was told, "Look! Some of the Israelites have come here tonight to spy out the* land." *So the king of Jericho sent this message to Rahab: "Bring out the men who came to you and entered your house, because **they have come to spy out the whole land."***

JOSH 6:17. *The city and all that is in it are to be devoted to the LORD. Only Rahab the prostitute and **all who are with her in her house shall be spared**, because she hid the spies we sent.*

JUDG 1:24-26. *the spies saw a man coming out of the city and they said to him, "Show us how to get into the city and we will see that you are treated well." So **he showed them, and they put the city to the sword but spared the man and his whole family.***

LUKE 20:20-26. *Keeping a close watch on him, they sent spies, who pretended to be honest. They hoped to catch Jesus in something he said so that they might hand him over to the power and authority of the governor. So the spies questioned him: "Teacher, we know that you speak and teach what is right, and that you do not show partiality but teach the way of God in accordance with the truth. Is it right for us to pay taxes to Caesar or not?" **He saw through their duplicity** and said to them, "Show me a denarius. Whose portrait and inscription are on it?" "Caesar's," they replied. He said to them, "Then give to Caesar what is Caesar's, and to God what is God's." **They were unable to trap him** in what he had said there in public. And astonished by his answer, they became silent.*

PHYSICAL ATTRIBUTE ADVANTAGES OF THE TONSILS: Produces antibodies to help fight foreign entities.

WITHOUT IT: I tend to be laid back, giving people the benefit of the doubt.

WITH IT: I deepen my relationships based on the individual fruits and earning my trust.

FOR COUPLE/GROUP:
Blood of Jesus Christ on our TONSILS so that the Word of God can Guard us in our relationship/s.

Blood of Jesus Christ on my:
VOCAL CORDS so that the Word of God can be Praised in my life.

REFERENCES:

PSALMS 113:2-3. *Let the name of the LORD be praised, both now and forevermore.* *From the rising of the sun to the place where it sets, the name of the LORD is to be praised.*

ISAIAH 63:7. *I will tell of the kindnesses of the LORD, the deeds for which he is to be praised, according to all the LORD has done for us —* yes, the many good things he has done for the house of Israel, according to his compassion and many kindnesses.

1 PET 4:11. If anyone speaks, he should do it as one speaking the very words of God. If anyone serves, he should do it with the strength *God provides, so that in all things God may be praised through Jesus Christ.* To him be the glory and the power for ever and ever. Amen.

PHYSICAL ATTRIBUTE ADVANTAGES OF THE VOCAL CHORDS: Sounds. Frequencies. Spoken Thought Amplifier.

WITHOUT IT: I lean towards praising myself more than others, let alone God.

WITH IT: I enjoy praising God anytime and anywhere.

FOR COUPLE/GROUP:

Blood of Jesus Christ on our VOCAL CORDS so that the Word of God can be Praised in our relationship/s.

Blood of Jesus Christ on my:

DIGESTIVE SYSTEM so that the Word of God can be Satisfied in my life.

REFERENCES:

PROV 30:15-16. "The leech has two daughters. 'Give! Give!' they cry. "*There are three things that are never satisfied, four that never say, 'Enough!': the grave, the barren womb, land,* which is never satisfied with water, *and fire,* which never says, 'Enough!'

PROV 27:20-21. *Death and Destruction are never satisfied, and neither are the eyes of man.* The crucible for silver and the furnace for gold, but man is tested by the praise he receives.

PROV 18:20. *From the fruit of his mouth a man's stomach is filled;* with the harvest from his lips he is *satisfied.*

HOSEA 13:6-7. **When I fed them, they were satisfied; when they were satisfied, they became proud;** *then they forgot me. So I will come upon them like a lion, like a leopard I will lurk by the path.*

ISAIAH 53:11-12. *After the suffering of his soul,* **he will see the light [of life] and be satisfied;** *by his knowledge my righteous servant will justify many, and he will bear their iniquities. Therefore I will give him a portion among the great, and he will divide the spoils with the strong, because he poured out his life unto death, and was numbered with the transgressors. For he bore the sin of many, and made intercession for the transgressors.*

PSALMS 22:26. **The poor will eat and be satisfied;** *they who seek the LORD will praise him — may your hearts live forever!*

PSALMS 17:15. *And I — in righteousness I will see your face;* **when I awake, I will be satisfied with seeing your likeness.**

PHYSICAL ATTRIBUTE ADVANTAGES OF THE DIGESTION SYSTEM: Satisfied. Harvests food for Body Utilization.

WITHOUT IT: No matter how much I eat I don't feel full.

WITH IT: I look back in my life, relationships and accomplishments and I am satisfied.

FOR COUPLE/GROUP:
Blood of Jesus Christ on our DIGESTIVE SYSTEMS so that the Word of God can be Satisfied in our relationship/s.

Blood of Jesus Christ on my:
INTESTINES so that the Word of God can be Absorbed in my life.

REFERENCES:

REV 3:3. *Remember, therefore,* **what you have received and heard; obey it, and repent.** *But if you do not wake up, I will come like a thief, and you will not know at what time I will come to you.*

1 JOHN 2:27. *As for you,* **the anointing you received from him remains in you,** *and you do not need anyone to teach you. But as his anointing teaches you about all things and as that anointing is real, not counterfeit-just as it has taught you, remain in him.*

1 PET 4:10-11. **Each one should use whatever gift he has received to serve others,** *faithfully administering God's grace in its various forms.*

HEB 10:32-37. ***Remember those earlier days after you had received the light, when you stood your ground in a great contest in the face of suffering.*** *Sometimes you were publicly exposed to insult and persecution; at other times you stood side by side with those who were so treated. You sympathized with those in prison and joyfully accepted the confiscation of your property, because you knew that you yourselves had better and lasting possessions. So do not throw away your confidence; it will be richly rewarded. You need to persevere so that when you have done the will of God you will receive what he has promised. For in just a very little while, "He who is coming will come and will not delay.*

HEB 6:15. *And so after waiting patiently,* ***Abraham received what was promised.***

1 THES 2:13-14. ***And we also thank God continually because, when you received the word of God,*** *which you heard from us,* ***you accepted it not as the word of men, but as it actually is, the word of God,*** *which is at work in you who believe.*

1 COR 15:3-4. ***For what I received I passed on to you as of first importance:*** *that Christ died for our sins according to the Scriptures, that he was buried, that he was raised on the third day according to the Scriptures,*

JOHN 10:18. ***No one takes it from me, but I lay it down of my own accord.*** *I have authority to lay it down and authority to take it up again. This command I received from my Father."*

MARK 11:24-25. *Therefore I tell you, whatever you ask for in prayer,* ***believe that you have received it, and it will be yours.***

MATT 10:7-8. *Heal the sick, raise the dead, cleanse those who have leprosy, drive out demons.* ***Freely you have received, freely give.***

PHYSICAL ATTRIBUTE ADVANTAGES OF THE INTESTINES:
Solids/Liquids/Energy Resource Harvester.

WITHOUT IT: I show no effect of pulling my "own weight"

WITH IT: I'm proactive in taking care of my challenges plus enough to help loved ones get established.

FOR COUPLE/GROUP:
Blood of Jesus Christ on our INTESTINES so that the Word of God can be Absorbed in our relationship/s.

Blood of Jesus Christ on my:
APPENDIX so that the Word of God can Restore my life.

REFERENCES:

DEUT 28:12-14. **The LORD will open the heavens, the storehouse of his county,** *to send rain on your land in season and to bless all the work of your hands. You will lend to many nations but will borrow from none. The LORD will make you the head, not the tail. If you pay attention to the commands of the LORD your God that I give you this day and carefully follow them, you will always be at the top, never at the bottom. Do not turn aside from any of the commands I give you today, to the right or to the left, following other gods and serving them.*

HOS 13:15. **even though he thrives among his brothers.** *An east wind from the LORD will come, blowing in from the desert; his spring will fail and his well dry up. His storehouse will be plundered of all its treasures.*

MAL 3:10-12. **Bring the whole tithe into the storehouse,** *that there may be food in my house. Test me in this," says the LORD Almighty, "and see if **I will not throw open the floodgates of heaven and pour out so much blessing that you will not have room enough for it.** I will prevent pests from devouring your crops, and the vines in your fields will not cast their fruit," says the LORD Almighty. "Then all the nations will call you blessed, for yours will be a delightful land," says the LORD Almighty.*

PHYSICAL ATTRIBUTE ADVANTAGES OF THE APPENDIX: Safe haven for good bacteria to hang out in the gut to repopulate digestion system when necessary.

WITHOUT IT: I tend to leave broken pieces, broken.

WITH IT: I favor being a peace maker/mediator between two conflicting entities.

FOR COUPLE/GROUP:

Blood of Jesus Christ on our APPENDIXES so that the Word of God can Restore our relationship/s.

Blood of Jesus Christ on my:

FAT so that the Word of God can Over Flow in my life.

REFERENCES:

GEN 4:4-5. *But Abel brought fat portions from some of the firstborn of his flock.* **The LORD looked with favor on Abel and his offering,**

GEN 41:2-4. **when out of the river there came up seven cows, sleek and fat, and they grazed among the reeds.** *After them, seven other cows, ugly and gaunt, came up out of the Nile and stood beside those on the riverbank.*

PROV 3:9-10. **Honor the LORD with your wealth,** with the first fruits of all your crops; **then your barns will be filled to overflowing,** and your vats will brim over with new wine.

2 COR 8:2-6. Out of the most severe trial, **their overflowing joy and their extreme poverty welled up in rich generosity.** For I testify that they gave as much as they were able, and even beyond their ability. Entirely on their own, they urgently pleaded with us for the privilege of sharing in this service to the saints. And they did not do as we expected, but they gave themselves first to the Lord and then to us in keeping with God's will.

PROV 1:29-31. Since they hated knowledge and did not choose to fear the LORD, since they would not accept my advice and spurned my rebuke, **they will eat the fruit of their ways and be filled with the fruit of their schemes.**

PROV 12:14. **From the fruit of his lips a man is filled with good things** as surely as the work of his hands rewards him.

DEUT 28:8. **The LORD will send a blessing on your barns and on everything you put your hand to.** The LORD your God will bless you in the land he is giving you.

LUKE 12:18-20. "Then he said, 'This is what I'll do. I will tear down my barns and build bigger ones, and there I will store all my grain and my goods. And **I'll say to myself, "You have plenty of good things laid up** for many years. Take life easy; eat, drink and be merry."' '"**But God said to him, 'You fool! This very night your life will be demanded from you.** Then who will get what you have prepared for yourself?'

PHYSICAL ATTRIBUTE ADVANTAGES OF FAT: Stored Food/Energy on stand by for anytime.

WITHOUT IT: I lean towards just having enough to get by. If I'm short I'll ask someone.

WITH IT: I have more than enough for myself, loved ones plus share with those who lack.

FOR COUPLE/GROUP:

Blood of Jesus Christ on our FAT so that the Word of God can Over Flow in our relationship/s.

Blood of Jesus Christ on my:

HEART so that the Word of God can be Treasured in my life.

REFERENCES:

1 TIM 6:17-19. *Command those who are rich in this present world not to be arrogant nor to put their hope in wealth, which is so uncertain, but to put their hope in God, who richly provides us with everything for our enjoyment. **Command them to do good, to be rich in good deeds, and to be generous and willing to share. In this way they will lay up treasure for themselves as a firm foundation for the coming age,** so that they may take hold of the life that is truly life.*

2 COR 4:7. *But we have this treasure in jars of clay to show that this all-surpassing power is from God and not from us.*

LUKE 12:33. *For where your treasure is, there your heart will be also.*

MATT 13:44. *"The kingdom of heaven is like treasure hidden in a field. When a man found it, he hid it again, and then in his joy went and sold all he had and bought that field.*

PROV 2:1. *My son, if you accept my words and **store up my commands within you,***

PROV 2:4-5. *and if you look for it as for silver and **search for it as for hidden treasure, then you will understand the fear of the LORD and find the knowledge of God.***

PROV 15:6. ***The house of the righteous contains great treasure,*** *but the income of the wicked brings them trouble.*

ISAIAH 33:6. *He will be the sure foundation for your times, **a rich store of salvation and wisdom and knowledge; the fear of the LORD is the key to this treasure.***

PHYSICAL ATTRIBUTE ADVANTAGES OF THE HEART: Delivers resources to network of systems.

WITHOUT IT: I'm fixated on accumulating temporary things and relationships.

WITH IT: I'm wired to accumulating spiritual treasures only found in Christ's Kingdom. God's Word is My treasure.

FOR COUPLE/GROUP:
Blood of Jesus Christ on our HEARTS so that the Word of God can be Treasured in our relationship/s.

Blood of Jesus Christ on my:
VEINS so that the Word of God can be Rooted in my life.

REFERENCES:

EPH 3:17-19. *so that Christ may dwell in your hearts through faith. And I pray that you, **being rooted and established in love**, may have power, together with all the saints, to grasp how wide and long and high and deep is the love of Christ, and to know this love that surpasses knowledge-that you may be filled to the measure of all the fullness of God.*

COL 2:6-10. *So then, just as you received Christ Jesus as Lord, continue to live in him, **rooted and built up in him**, strengthened in the faith as you were taught, and overflowing with thankfulness. See to it that no one takes you captive through hollow and deceptive philosophy, which depends on human tradition and the basic principles of this world rather than on Christ. For in Christ all the fullness of the Deity lives in bodily form, and you have been given fullness in Christ, who is the head over every power and authority.*

MATT 13:20-21. *The one who received the seed that fell on rocky places is the man who hears the word and at once receives it with joy. **But since he has no root, he lasts only a short time.** When trouble or persecution comes because of the word, he quickly falls away.*

PHYSICAL ATTRIBUTE ADVANTAGES OF THE VEINS: Body Resource Output Endurance. Perseverance. Deeper vein/root system equals longer perseverance.

WITHOUT IT: It doesn't take much for me to crack under pressure.

WITH IT: No fear of the one who can hurt the body because I fear the one who can destroy both the body and spirit.

FOR COUPLE/GROUP:
Blood of Jesus Christ on our VEINS so that the Word of God can be Rooted in our relationship/s.

Blood of Jesus Christ on my:
BLOOD so that the Word of God can be Perpetuated in my life.

REFERENCES:

PSALMS 45:17. ***I will perpetuate your memory through all generations**; therefore the nations will praise you for ever and ever.*

DEUT 12:23-25. *But be sure you do not eat the blood, **because the blood is the life**, and you must not eat the life with the meat. You must not eat the blood;*

pour it out on the ground like water. **Do not eat it, so that it may go well with you and your children after you,** *because you will be doing what is right in the eyes of the LORD.*

DEUT 30:15-16. *See, I set before you today life and prosperity, death and destruction. For* **I command you today to love the LORD your God, to walk in his ways, and to keep his commands, decrees and laws; then you will live and increase,** *and the LORD your God will bless you in the land you are entering to possess.*

PSALMS 119:25. *I am laid low in the dust;* **preserve my life according to your word.**

PSALMS 119:115. *Defend my cause and redeem me;* **preserve my life according to your promise.**

MATT 10:39. *Whoever finds his life will lose it,* **and whoever loses his life for my sake will find it.**

LUKE 21:19. **By standing firm you will gain life.**

JOHN 3:16. *"For God so loved the world that he gave his one and only Son, that* **whoever believes in him shall not perish but have eternal life.**

JOHN 1:3-4. *Through him all things were made; without him nothing was made that has been made.* **In him was life, and that life was the light of men.**

JOHN 14:6-7 *Jesus answered, "***I am the way and the truth and the life.** *No one comes to the Father except through me.*

PHYSICAL ATTRIBUTE ADVANTAGES OF THE BLOOD: Glue that holds body and soul together. Temporary connection, that provides a placenta as housing for an eternal entity. Deliverance option, that can be utilized. Delivering Life.

WITHOUT IT: Insecure in who I am.

WITH IT: My hope sustains me.

FOR COUPLE/GROUP:
Blood of Jesus Christ on our BLOOD so that the Word of God can be Perpetuated in our relationship/s.

Blood of Jesus Christ on my:
KIDNEYS so that the Word of God can be Refined in my life.

REFERENCES:

JOB 16:12-14. *All was well with me, but he shattered me; he seized me by the neck and crushed me. He has made me his target; his archers surround me. **Without pity, he pierces my kidneys** and spills my gall on the ground. Again and again he bursts upon me; he rushes at me like a warrior.*

JOB 28:12-13. ***"But where can wisdom be found?** Where does understanding dwell? Man does not comprehend its worth; it cannot be found in the land of the living.*

PSALMS 12:6. **And the words of the LORD are flawless, like silver refined in a furnace of clay, purified seven times.**

PSALMS 66:10. *For you, O God, tested us; **you refined us like silver.***

ISAIAH 48:10-11. *See, **I have refined you**, though not as silver; **I have tested you in the furnace of affliction.** For my own sake, for my own sake, I do this. How can I let myself be defamed? I will not yield my glory to another.*

DAN 11:35. **Some of the wise will stumble, so that they may be refined**, *purified and made spotless until the time of the end, for it will still come at the appointed time.*

DAN 12:9-10. **Many will be purified, made spotless and refined**, *but the wicked will continue to be wicked. None of the wicked will understand, but those who are wise will understand.*

1 PET 1:6-9. *These have come so that your faith-of greater worth than gold, **which perishes even though refined by fire-may be proved genuine and may result in praise, glory and honor when Jesus Christ is revealed**. Though you have not seen him, you love him; and even though you do not see him now, you believe in him and are filled with an inexpressible and glorious joy, for you are receiving the goal of your faith, the salvation of your souls.*

PHYSICAL ATTRIBUTE ADVANTAGES OF THE KIDNEYS: Harvests Excess Resources.

WITHOUT IT: I tend to be a "pack rat" keeping everything throwing/giving away nothing.

WITH IT: I tend to be a good steward with the entities God has given me.

FOR COUPLE/GROUP:

Blood of Jesus Christ on our KIDNEYS so that the Word of God can be Refined in our relationship/s.

Blood of Jesus Christ on my:

BLADDER so that the Word of God can provide Over Flow Storage my life.

REFERENCES:

PSALMS 65:12. **The grasslands of the desert overflow**; *the hills are clothed with gladness.*

PSALMS 65:11. *You crown the year with your bounty,* **and your carts overflow with abundance.**

PSALMS 119:171. **May my lips overflow with praise,** *for you teach me your decrees.*

LAM 1:16. **"This is why I weep and my eyes overflow with tears.** *No one is near to comfort me, no one to restore my spirit. My children are destitute because the enemy has prevailed."*

JOEL 2:24. *The threshing floors will be filled with grain;* **the vats will overflow with new wine and oil.**

ZECH 1:17. *"Proclaim further: This is what the LORD Almighty says:* **'My towns will again overflow with prosperity,** *and the LORD will again comfort Zion and choose Jerusalem.'"*

MATT 12:34. *You brood of vipers, how can you who are evil say anything good?* **For out of the overflow of the heart the mouth speaks.**

ROM 5:15. *But the gift is not like the trespass. For if the many died by the trespass of the one man, how much more did God's grace and* **the gift that came by the grace of the one man, Jesus Christ, overflow to the many!**

ROM 15:13. *May the God of hope fill you with all joy and peace as you trust in him,* **so that you may overflow with hope by the power of the Holy Spirit.**

2 COR 4:15. *All this is for your benefit, so that the* **grace that is reaching more and more people may cause thanksgiving to overflow to the glory of God.**

PHYSICAL ATTRIBUTE ADVANTAGES OF THE BLADDER: Holding Container for Excess Liquids.

WITHOUT IT: I lean towards not letting people give me their extra baggage/problems.

WITH IT: I tend to organize systems to maximize flow affecting people directly or indirectly.

FOR COUPLE/GROUP:

Blood of Jesus Christ on our BLADDERS so that the Word of God can provide Over Flow Storages in our relationship/s.

Blood of Jesus Christ on my:

LIVER so that the Word of God can be Input Resource Balancer in my life.

REFERENCES:

JOB 20:25-29. *He pulls it out of his back, the gleaming point out of his liver.* Terrors will come over him; total darkness lies in wait for his treasures. A fire unfanned will consume him and devour what is left in his tent. The heavens will expose his guilt; the earth will rise up against him. A flood will carry off his house, rushing waters on the day of God's wrath. Such is the fate God allots the wicked, the heritage appointed for them by God."

PROV 7:23. *till an arrow pierces his liver,* like a bird darting into a snare, little knowing it will cost him his life.

2 COR 8:1-6. Out of the most severe trial, their overflowing joy and their extreme poverty welled up in rich generosity. For I testify that they gave as much as they were able, and even beyond their ability. Entirely on their own, they urgently pleaded with us for the privilege of sharing in this service to the saints. *And they did not do as we expected, but they gave themselves first to the Lord and then to us in keeping with God's will.*

ROMANS 5:16-17. *For if, by the trespass of the one man, death reigned through that one man, how much more will those who receive God's abundant provision of grace and of the gift of righteousness reign in life through the one man, Jesus Christ.*

PROV 12:11. *He who works his land will have abundant food*, but he who chases fantasies lacks judgment.

DEUT 28:9-11. The LORD will establish you as his holy people, as he promised you on oath, *if you keep the commands of the LORD your God and walk in his ways. Then all the peoples on earth will see that you are called by the name of the LORD, and they will fear you.* The LORD will grant you abundant prosperity — in the fruit of your womb, the young of your livestock and the crops of your ground — in the land he swore to your forefathers to give you.

1 TIM 1:14. *The grace of our Lord was poured out on me abundantly, along with the faith and love that are in Christ Jesus.*

PHYSICAL ATTRIBUTE ADVANTAGES OF THE LIVER: Balances Fluxuations in Nutritional Inputs.

WITHOUT IT: I have a hard time handling more than one thing at a time.

WITH IT: Easy for me to properly prioritize life's events and relationships in a balanced perspective.

FOR COUPLE/GROUP:
Blood of Jesus Christ on our LIVERS so that the Word of God can be Input Resource Balancers in our relationship/s.

Blood of Jesus Christ on my:
PANCREAS so that the Word of God can be Energized in my life.

REFERENCES:

COL 1:28-29. *We proclaim him, admonishing and teaching everyone with all wisdom, so that we may present everyone perfect in Christ.* **To this end I labor, struggling with all his energy, which so powerfully works in me.**

MATT 25:26-27. *"His master replied, 'You wicked, lazy servant! So* **you knew that I harvest where I have not sown** *and gather where I have not scattered seed? Well then, you should have put my money on deposit with the bankers, so that when I returned I would have received it back with interest.*

HEB 6:11-12. **We want each of you to show this same diligence to the very end, in order to make your hope sure.** *We do not want you to become lazy, but to imitate those who through faith and patience inherit what has been promised.*

PHYSICAL ATTRIBUTE ADVANTAGES OF THE PANCREAS: Balances Fluxuations in Energy Inputs.

WITHOUT IT: I hurry to start a new project and then lose interest in finishing it.

WITH IT: Love life in balanced way.

FOR COUPLE/GROUP:
Blood of Jesus Christ on our PANCREASES so that the Word of God can be Energized in our relationship/s.

Blood of Jesus Christ on my:

LUNGS so that the Word of God can be Baptized in the Holy Spirit in my life.

REFERENCES:

MATT 3:11-12. *"I baptize you with water for repentance. But after me will come one who is more powerful than I, whose sandals I am not fit to carry.* **He will baptize you with the Holy Spirit and with fire.** *His winnowing fork is in his hand, and he will clear his threshing*

MARK 16:16-18. *Whoever believes and is baptized will be saved, but whoever does not believe will be condemned.* **And these signs will accompany those who believe:** *In my name they will drive out demons; they will speak in new tongues; they will pick up snakes with their hands; and when they drink deadly poison, it will not hurt them at all; they will place their hands on sick people, and they will get well."*

LUKE 12:10. *And everyone who speaks a word against the Son of Man will be forgiven,* **but anyone who blasphemes against the Holy Spirit will not be forgiven.**

PHYSICAL ATTRIBUTE ADVANTAGES OF THE LUNGS: Air/Gas Fuel harvester for the body to maximize tangible resources for the body systems.

WITHOUT IT: I tend to pass out on noted events in my life.

WITH IT: Operating in gifts and fruits of the Spirit.

FOR COUPLE/GROUP:

Blood of Jesus Christ on our LUNGS so that the Word of God can be Baptized in the Holy Spirit in our relationship/s.

Blood of Jesus Christ on my:

RESPIRATORY SYSTEM so that the Word of God can Breath in my life.

REFERENCES:

ACTS 17:25. *And he is not served by human hands, as if he needed anything, because* **he himself gives all men life and breath** *and everything else.*

EZEK 37:9-10. *Then he said to me, "Prophesy to the breath; prophesy, son of man, and say to it, 'This is what **the Sovereign LORD says: Come from the four winds, O breath, and breathe into these slain, that they may live**.'" So I prophesied as he commanded me, and breath entered them; they came to life and stood up on their feet-a vast army.*

PSALMS 33:6. *By the word of the LORD were the heavens made, **their starry host by the breath of his mouth**.*

JOB 34:14-15. ***If it were his intention and he withdrew his spirit and breath**, all mankind would perish together and man would return to the dust.*

1 JOHN 5:12. ***He who has the Son has life;** he who does not have the Son of God does not have life.*

PHYSICAL ATTRIBUTE ADVANTAGES OF THE RESPIRATORY SYSTEM: Processing Air Input Output System.

WITHOUT IT: I lean towards avoiding the spiritual concepts of life.

WITH IT: I comprehend spiritual tools and how to harness them to acquire spiritual treasures.

FOR COUPLE/GROUP:

Blood of Jesus Christ on our RESPIRATORY SYSTEMS so that the Word of God can Breath in our relationship/s.

Blood of Jesus Christ on my:

IMMUNE SYSTEM so that the Word of God can Resist in my life.

REFERENCES:

PROV 28:4. *Those who forsake the law praise the wicked, **but those who keep the law resist them**.*

DAN 11:32. *With flattery he will corrupt those who have violated the covenant, **but the people who know their God will firmly resist him**.*

LUKE 21:15. ***For I will give you words and wisdom that none of your adversaries will be able to resist or contradict**.*

ACTS 7:51-52. *"You stiff-necked people, with uncircumcised hearts and ears! You are just like your fathers: **You always resist the Holy Spirit!***

JAMES 4:7. *Submit yourselves, then, to God. **Resist the devil, and he will flee from you**.*

PHYSICAL ATTRIBUTE ADVANTAGES OF THE IMMUNE SYSTEM:
Monitors, produces and defends the body from outside intruders.

WITHOUT IT: I lean towards believing "maybe it's not as bad as they say it is."

WITH IT: I check my relationships and assets conditions daily to make adjustments to keep them in good condition.

FOR COUPLE/GROUP:
Blood of Jesus Christ on our IMMUNE SYSTEMS so that the Word of God can Resist in our relationship/s.

Blood of Jesus Christ on my:
REPRODUCTIVE SYSTEM so that the Word of God can Multiply in my life.

REFERENCES:
GEN 1:28. *God blessed them and said to them, "**Be fruitful and increase in number;** fill the earth and subdue it. Rule over the fish of the sea and the birds of the air and over every living creature that moves on the ground."*

JOHN 15:2. *He cuts off every branch in me that bears no fruit, while **every branch that does bear fruit he prunes so that it will be even more fruitful.***

JERE 4:26. ***I looked, and the fruitful land was a desert;*** *all its towns lay in ruins before the LORD, before his fierce anger.*

DEUT 7:21-22. *The LORD your God will drive out those nations before you, little by little. **You will not be allowed to eliminate them all at once, or the wild animals will multiply around you.***

LEV 26:21. *"**If** you remain hostile toward me and **refuse to listen to me, I will multiply your afflictions** seven times over, as your sins deserve.*

EXO 7:3-4. *But **I will harden Pharaoh's heart, and though I multiply my miraculous signs and wonders in Egypt,** he will not listen to you. Then I will lay my hand on Egypt and with mighty acts of judgment I will bring out my divisions, my people the Israelites.*

PHYSICAL ATTRIBUTE ADVANTAGES OF THE REPRODUCTIVE SYSTEM:
Multiples. Accelerates Networking Output. Bigger Networks are needed for Bigger Projects. Celebrations are more colorful. Audiences to enjoy live expressions.

WITHOUT IT: Not interested in multiplication if it's going to cost me time and money.

WITH IT: I bring the best out in me through quality multiplication.

FOR COUPLE/GROUP:
Blood of Jesus Christ on our REPRODUCTIVE SYSTEMS so that the Word of God can Multiply in our relationship/s.

Blood of Jesus Christ on my:
MUSCLES so that the Word of God can be Strengthen in my life.

REFERENCES:

JOB 10:10-12. *Did you not pour me out like milk and curdle me like cheese, **clothe me with skin and flesh and knit me together** with bones and sinews? You gave me life and showed me kindness, and in your providence watched over my spirit.*

PSALMS 119:28. *My soul is weary with sorrow; **strengthen me according to your word.***

ISAIAH 41:10. *So do not fear, for I am with you; do not be dismayed, for I am your God. **I will strengthen you and help you**; I will uphold you with my righteous right hand.*

ISAIAH 58:11. ***The LORD will guide you always;** he will satisfy your needs in a sun-scorched land **and will strengthen your frame.** You will be like a well-watered garden, like a spring whose waters never fail.*

2 THES 3:3. *But the Lord is faithful, and **he will strengthen and protect you from the evil one.***

2 THES 2:17. ***encourage your hearts and strengthen you in every good deed and word.***

EPH 3:16. ***I pray** that out of his glorious riches **he may strengthen you with power through his Spirit in your inner being,***

ZECH 10:12. ***I will strengthen them in the LORD** and in his name they will walk,"* declares the LORD.

EZEK 34:16. *I will search for the lost and bring back the strays. **I will bind up the injured and strengthen the weak,** but the sleek and the strong I will destroy. I will shepherd the flock with justice.*

PHYSICAL ATTRIBUTE ADVANTAGES OF THE MUSCLES: Strength, Limber/Flexibility and Shape.

WITHOUT IT: I lack the flexibility and strength to handle the challenges that come my way. I find myself going out of my way to get others to face them for me.

WITH IT: I embrace my challenge with expectations of discovering new solutions that will make me more limber at handling future challenges. Enhances my mental muscle shape.

FOR COUPLE/GROUP:
Blood of Jesus Christ on our MUSCLES so that the Word of God can be Strengthen in our relationship/s.

Blood of Jesus Christ on my:
BODY so that the Word of God can Contain the Holy Spirit in my life.

REFERENCES:

2 COR 7:1. *Since we have these promises, dear friends,* **let us purify ourselves from everything that contaminates body** *and spirit, perfecting holiness out of reverence for God.*

ROMANS 8:10-11. **But if Christ is in you, your body is dead because of sin,** *yet your spirit is alive because of righteousness. And if the Spirit of him who raised Jesus from the dead is living in you, he who raised Christ from the dead will also give life to your mortal bodies through his Spirit, who lives in you.*

1 COR 6:19-20. **Do you not know that your body is a temple of the Holy Spirit,** *who is in you, whom you have received from God? You are not your own; you were bought at a price. Therefore honor God with your body.*

TITUS 3:5-6. **he saved us, not because of righteous things we had done, but because of his mercy.** *He saved us through the washing of rebirth and renewal by the Holy Spirit,*

EPH 4:29-32. *Do not let any unwholesome talk come out of your mouths, but only what is helpful for building others up according to their needs, that it may benefit those who listen.* **And do not grieve the Holy Spirit of God, with whom you were sealed for the day of redemption.** *Get rid of all bitterness, rage and anger, brawling and slander, along with every form of malice. Be kind and compassionate to one another,* **forgiving each other,** *just as in Christ God forgave you.*

ACTS 1:8. *But you will receive power when the Holy Spirit comes on you; and* **you will be my witnesses** *in Jerusalem, and in all Judea and Samaria, and to the ends of the earth."*

PHYSICAL ATTRIBUTE ADVANTAGES OF THE BODY: Container of variety of entities, big picture and sheppard/manager.

WITHOUT IT: I lose sight of why I was created. I lean towards being an introvert.

WITH IT: I enter into a friendship relationship with God.

FOR COUPLE/GROUP:

Blood of Jesus Christ on our BODIES so that the Word of God can Contain the Holy Spirit in our relationship/s.

Blood of Jesus Christ on my:

REST so that the Word of God can create Complete Rest in my life.

REFERENCES:

EXO 16:23. *He said to them, "This is what the LORD commanded:* **'Tomorrow is to be a day of rest, a holy Sabbath to the LORD.** *So bake what you want to bake and boil what you want to boil. Save whatever is left and keep it until morning.'"*

EXO 34:21. *"Six days you shall labor, but* **on the seventh day you shall rest***; even during the plowing season and harvest you must rest.*

LEV 16:31. **It is a Sabbath of rest, and you must deny yourselves***; it is a lasting ordinance.*

LEV 23:3. *"'There are six days when you may work, but* **the seventh day is a Sabbath of rest, a day of sacred assembly.** *You are not to do any work; wherever you live, it is a Sabbath to the LORD.*

DEUT 25:19. *When* **the LORD your God gives you rest from all the enemies around you** *in the land he is giving you to possess as an inheritance, you shall blot out the memory of Amalek from under heaven. Do not forget!*

NEH 9:28. **"But as soon as they were at rest,** *they again did what was evil in your sight. Then you abandoned them to the hand of their enemies so that they ruled over them. And when they cried out to you again, you heard from heaven, and in your compassion you delivered them time after time.*

JOB 24:23. *He may let them rest in a feeling of security,* but his eyes are on their ways.

PSALMS 33:22. *May your unfailing love rest upon us,* O LORD, even as we put our hope in you.

PSALMS 62:1. For the director of music. For Jeduthun. A psalm of David. *My soul finds rest in God alone;* my salvation comes from him.

PROV 21:16. *A man who strays from the path of understanding comes to rest in the company of the dead.*

ISA 14:7. *All the lands are at rest and at peace;* they break into singing.

ISA 30:15. This is what the Sovereign LORD, the Holy One of Israel, says: "In repentance and *rest is your salvation,* in quietness and trust is your strength, but you would have none of it.

ZECH 1:11. And they reported to the angel of the LORD, who was standing among the myrtle trees. *"We have gone throughout the earth and found the whole world at rest and in peace."*

MATT 11:28-30. "Come to me, all you who are weary and burdened, and *I will give you rest.* Take my yoke upon you and learn from me, for I am gentle and humble in heart, and you will find rest for your souls.

HEB 4:10-11. *for anyone who enters God's rest also rests from his own work,* just as God did from his. Let us, therefore, make every effort to enter that rest, so that no one will fall by following their example of disobedience.

REV 14:13. Then I heard a voice from heaven say, "Write: Blessed are the dead who die in the Lord *from now on.*" "Yes," says the Spirit, *"they will rest from their labor, for their deeds will follow them."*

PHYSICAL ATTRIBUTE ADVANTAGES OF REST: Re-energizes body. Creativity Fuel. Maximized Rest equals Maximized Life Ingredients.

WITHOUT IT: Even though I rest I don't feel rested. Never enough time in the day to get done the items need to do.

WITH IT: The degree I seek harmony with God and His Kingdom is the degree of rest I enter into.

FOR COUPLE/GROUP:

Blood of Jesus Christ on our REST so that the Word of God can Create Complete Rest in our relationship/s.

Blood of Jesus Christ on my:

SOUL so that the Word of God can be Resurrected in my life.

REFERENCES:

DEUT 4:29-30. *But if from there you seek the LORD your God,* **you will find him if you look for him with all your heart and with all your soul.**

DEUT 6:5. **Love the LORD your God with** *all your heart and with* **all your soul** *and with all your strength.*

DEUT 10:12. *And now, O Israel, what does the LORD your God ask of you but to fear the LORD your God, to walk in all his ways, to love him,* **to serve the LORD your God with** *all your heart and with* **all your soul,**

JOB 33:28. **He redeemed my soul from going down to the pit,** *and I will live to enjoy the light.'*

PSALMS 6:3. **My soul is in anguish.** *How long, O LORD, how long?*

PSALMS 19:7. **The law of the LORD is perfect, reviving the soul.**

PSALMS 23:3. **he restores my soul.** *He guides me in paths of righteousness for his name's sake.*

PSALMS 31:9. *Be merciful to me, O LORD, for I am in distress; my eyes grow weak with sorrow,* **my soul and my body with grief.**

PSALMS 35:9. **Then my soul will rejoice in the LORD** *and delight in his salvation.*

PSALMS 42:2. *My soul thirsts for God, for the living God. When can I go and meet with God?*

PSALMS 62:1. *For the director of music. For Jeduthun. A psalm of David.* **My soul finds rest in God alone;** *my salvation comes from him.*

PSALMS 88:3. **For my soul is full of trouble** *and my life draws near the grave.*

PSALMS 108:1. *My heart is steadfast, O God;* **I will sing and make music with all my soul.**

PSALMS 119:28. **My soul is weary with sorrow;** *strengthen me according to your word.*

PROV 2:10-11. *For wisdom will enter your heart, and* **knowledge will be pleasant to your soul.** *Discretion will protect you, and understanding will guard you.*

PROV 13:19. **A longing fulfilled is sweet to the soul,** *but fools detest turning from evil.*

PROV 16:24. **Pleasant words are a honeycomb, sweet to the soul** *and healing to the bones.*

PROV 19:8. **He who gets wisdom loves his own soul;** *he who cherishes understanding prospers.*

PROV 24:14. **Know also that wisdom is sweet to your soul;** *if you find it, there is a future hope for you, and your hope will not be cut off.*

MATT 10:28. *Do not be afraid of those who kill the body but cannot kill the soul.* **Rather, be afraid of the One who can destroy both soul and body in hell.**

MATT 16:26. *What good will it be for a man if he gains the whole world, yet forfeits his soul? Or* **what can a man give in exchange for his soul?**

HEB 4:12-13. **For the word of God is living and active.** *Sharper than any double-edged sword,* **it penetrates even to dividing soul and spirit,** *joints and marrow; it judges the thoughts and attitudes of the heart.*

1 PET 2:11-12. *Dear friends, I urge you, as aliens and strangers in the world, to* **abstain from sinful desires, which war against your soul.**

PHYSICAL ATTRIBUTE ADVANTAGES OF THE SOUL: Connecting with Physical Life harmoniously.

WITHOUT IT: I tend to look at life being more chemical.

WITH IT: I embrace the belief that life is spiritual and desire to connect to it.

FOR COUPLE/GROUP:
Blood of Jesus Christ on our SOULS so that the Word of God can be Resurrected in our relationship/s.

Blood of Jesus Christ on my:
SPIRIT so that the Word of God can Save Me from Death in my life.

REFERENCES:

EXO 31:3-5 3. *and* **I have filled him with the Spirit of God**, *with skill, ability and knowledge in all kinds of crafts — to make artistic designs for work in gold, silver and bronze, to cut and set stones, to work in wood, and to engage in all kinds of craftsmanship.*

NUM 11:17. *I will come down and speak with you there, and* **I will take of the Spirit that is on you and put the Spirit on them.** *They will help you carry the burden of the people so that you will not have to carry it alone.*

PSALMS 34:18. *The LORD* is close to the brokenhearted and *saves those who are crushed in spirit.*

PSALMS 104:30. *When you send your Spirit,* they are created, and *you renew the face of the earth.*

PSALMS 146:4. *When their spirit departs, they return to the ground;* on that very day their plans come to nothing.

PROV 15:4. The tongue that brings healing is a tree of life, but *a deceitful tongue crushes the spirit.*

PROV 15:13. A happy heart makes the face cheerful, but *heartache crushes the spirit.*

PROV 16:18-19. Pride goes before destruction, *a haughty spirit before a fall. Better to be lowly in spirit* and among the oppressed than to share plunder with the proud.

PROV 17:22. A cheerful heart is good medicine, but *a crushed spirit dries up the bones.*

PROV 18:14. *A man's spirit sustains him in sickness,* but *a crushed spirit who can bear?*

PROV 20:27-28. *The lamp of the LORD searches the spirit of a man;* it searches out his inmost being. Love and faithfulness keep a king safe; through love his throne is made secure.

PROV 25:13. Like the coolness of snow at harvest time is *a trustworthy messenger to those who send him; he refreshes the spirit of his masters.*

PROV 29:23. A man's pride brings him low, but *a man of lowly spirit gains honor.*

ZECH 4:6. So he said to me, "This is the word of the LORD to Zerubbabel: *'Not by might nor by power, but by my Spirit,'* says the LORD Almighty.

MARK 14:38. Watch and pray so that you will not fall into temptation. *The spirit is willing,* but the body is weak."

LUKE 11:24-26. *"When an evil spirit comes out of a man, it goes through arid places seeking rest and does not find it.* Then it says, 'I will return to the house I left.' When it arrives, it finds the house swept clean and put in order. Then it goes and takes seven other spirits more wicked than itself, and they go in and live there. And the final condition of that man is worse than the first."

LUKE 12:12. for *the Holy Spirit will teach you at that time* what you should say

LUKE 23:45-46. Jesus called out with a loud voice, *"Father, into your hands I commit my spirit."* When he had said this, he breathed his last.

JOHN 3:5-8. Jesus answered, "I tell you the truth, *no one can enter the kingdom of God unless he is born of water and the Spirit.* Flesh gives birth to flesh, but *the Spirit gives birth to spirit.* You should not be surprised at my saying,

'You must be born again.' The wind blows wherever it pleases. You hear its sound, but you cannot tell where it comes from or where it is going. So it is with everyone born of the Spirit."

JOHN 6:63-64. **The Spirit gives life**; the flesh counts for nothing. **The words I have spoken to you are spirit** and they are life.

JOHN 14:16-18. **the Spirit of truth**. The world cannot accept him, because it neither sees him nor knows him. But you know him, for he lives with you and will be in you.

JOHN 14:26-27. But **the Counselor, the Holy Spirit**, whom the Father will send in my name, **will teach you all things** and will remind you of everything I have said to you.

ROMANS 8:9. You, however, are controlled not by the sinful nature but by the Spirit, if the Spirit of God lives in you. And if **anyone does not have the Spirit of Christ, he does not belong to Christ.**

ROMANS 8:10-11. But if Christ is in you, your body is dead because of sin, yet your spirit is alive because of righteousness. And **if the Spirit of him who raised Jesus from the dead is living in you,** he who raised Christ from the dead **will also give life to your mortal bodies through his Spirit**, who lives in you.

ROMANS 8:16-17. **The Spirit himself testifies with our spirit that we are God's children.** Now if we are children, then we are heirs-heirs of God and co-heirs with Christ, if indeed we share in his sufferings in order that we may also share in his glory.

1 COR 6:17. **But he who unites himself with the Lord is one with him in spirit**

2 TIM 1:7. **For God did not give us a spirit of timidity, but a spirit of power**, of love and of self-discipline.

1 JOHN 4:2-3. This is how you can recognize the Spirit of God: **Every spirit that acknowledges that Jesus Christ has come in the flesh is from God**, but every spirit that does not acknowledge Jesus is not from God. This is the spirit of the antichrist, which you have heard is coming and even now is already in the world.

PHYSICAL ATTRIBUTE ADVANTAGES OF THE SPIRIT: Connecting with Spiritual Life Harmoniously.

WITHOUT IT: I wrestle with the concept, is there a God or not? Is there a Heaven or Hell?

WITH IT: God and I are in one mind. I'm experiencing a peace that passes all understanding.

FOR COUPLE/GROUP:
Blood of Jesus Christ on our SPIRITS so that the Word of God can Save Us from Death in our relationship/s.

Blood of Jesus Christ on my:
WORDS so that the Word of God will be Meaningful in my life.

REFERENCES:

DEUT 32:2 *Let my teaching fall like rain and **my words descend like dew**, like showers on new grass, like abundant rain on tender plants.*

JOB 13:17 **Listen carefully to my words; let your ears take in what I say.**

JOB 24:25 *"If this is not so, **who can** prove me false and **reduce my words to nothing?"***

JOB 29:22-23 *After I had spoken, they spoke no more; my words fell gently on their ears.* **They** *waited for me as for showers and **drank in my words as the spring rain.***

PSALMS 50:17 *You hate my instruction and **cast my words behind you.***

PSALMS 56:5 **All day long they twist my words;** *they are always plotting to harm me.*

EZEK 12:28 *"Therefore say to them, 'This is what the Sovereign LORD says:* **None of my words will be delayed any longer;** *whatever I say will be fulfilled, declares the Sovereign LORD.'"*

LUKE 6:47-48 **I will show you what he is like who comes to me and hears my words and puts them into practice.**

JOHN 15:7 **If** *you remain in me and **my words remain in you, ask whatever you wish, and it will be given you.***

PHYSICAL ATTRIBUTE ADVANTAGES OF MY WORDS: Catalysts that moves entities in any direction.

WITHOUT IT: I tend to isolate myself. Twist relationships. Pit one against another. Testing.

WITH IT: I have a drive to share myself. I chose depth over surface in relationship bonding. Supporting.

FOR COUPLE/GROUP:
Blood of Jesus Christ on our WORDS so that the Word of God will be Meaningful in our relationship/s.

Blood of Jesus Christ on my:
The GROUND MY FEET WALK ON so that the Word of God can Bear Abundant Fruit in my life.

REFERENCES:

EPH 6:13-18. **Therefore put on the full armor of God**, so that when the day of evil comes, **you may be able to stand your ground**, and after you have done everything, to stand. Stand firm then, with the belt of truth buckled around your waist, with the breastplate of righteousness in place, and with your feet fitted with the readiness that comes from the gospel of peace. In addition to all this, take up the shield of faith, with which you can extinguish all the flaming arrows of the evil one. Take the helmet of salvation and the sword of the Spirit, which is the word of God. And pray in the Spirit on all occasions with all kinds of prayers and requests. With this in mind, be alert and always keep on praying for all the saints.

ACTS 7:33. "Then the Lord said to him, **'Take off your sandals; the place where you are standing is holy ground.**

JOHN 18:5-6. **When Jesus said, "I am he," they drew back and fell to the ground.**

JOHN 12:24-25. I tell you the truth, unless a kernel of wheat falls to the ground and dies, it remains only a single seed. **But if it dies, it produces many seeds.**

JOHN 8:8. **Again he stooped down and wrote on the ground.**

ZECH 8:12-13. "The seed will grow well, the vine will yield its fruit, **the ground will produce its crops,** and the heavens will drop their dew. **I will give all these things as an inheritance** to the remnant of this people.

AMOS 2:15. **The archer will not stand his ground,** the fleet-footed soldier will not get away, and the horseman will not save his life.

HOSEA 10:12-13. **Sow for yourselves righteousness, reap the fruit of unfailing love, and break up your unplowed ground; for it is time to seek the LORD, until he comes and showers righteousness on you.** But you have planted wickedness, you have reaped evil, you have eaten the fruit of deception. Because you have depended on your own strength and on your many warriors,

PSALMS 143:10. Teach me to do your will, for you are my God; **may your good Spirit lead me on level ground.**

PSALMS 73:18-19. **Surely you place them on slippery ground;** you cast them down to ruin. How suddenly are they destroyed, completely swept away by terrors!

DEUT 28:23-24. *The sky over your head will be bronze, **the ground beneath you iron**. The LORD will turn the rain of your country into dust and powder; it will come down from the skies until you are destroyed.*

LEV 18:28. *And **if you defile the land, it will vomit you out** as it vomited out the nations that were before you.*

PHYSICAL ATTRIBUTE ADVANTAGES OF the GROUND MY FEET WALK ON: Yield Versus Time Spent Obtaining it.

WITHOUT IT: I tend to step into traps and spend a lot of time at my fork in the road choices.

WITH IT: My God and Enemies are at peace with me.

FOR COUPLE/GROUP:

Blood of Jesus Christ on the Ground Our Feet Walk On so that the Word of God can Bear Abundant Fruit in our relationship/s.

Blood of Jesus Christ on my:

BED so that the Word of God can be Undefiled in my life.

REFERENCES:

JOB 7:13-14. *When **I think my bed will comfort me and my couch will ease my complaint,** even then you frighten me with dreams and terrify me with visions,*

PSALMS 36:4. ***Even on his bed he plots evil**; he commits himself to a sinful course and does not reject what is wrong.*

PSALMS 41:1-3. *Blessed is he who has regard for the weak; the LORD delivers him in times of trouble. The LORD will protect him and preserve his life; he will bless him in the land and not surrender him to the desire of his foes. **The LORD will sustain him on his sickbed and restore him from his bed of illness.***

PSALMS 139:8. *If I go up to the heavens, you are there; **if I make my bed in the depths, you are there.***

PROV 22:27. ***if you lack the means to pay, your very bed will be snatched from under you.***

MARK 4:21-23. *He said to them, **"Do you bring in a lamp to put it under a bowl or a bed?** Instead, don't you put it on its stand? For whatever is hidden is meant to be disclosed, and whatever is concealed is meant to be brought out into the open. If anyone has ears to hear, let him hear."*

REV 2:22-23. *So **I will cast her on a bed of suffering**, and I will make those who commit adultery with her suffer intensely, unless they repent of her ways.*

HEB 13:4-5. **Marriage should be honored by all, and the marriage bed kept pure,** *for God will judge the adulterer and all the sexually immoral.*

PHYSICAL ATTRIBUTE ADVANTAGES OF THE BED: Spouse helps build up my house. Doubles Efforts. Pleasure without strife.

WITHOUT IT: My spouse is reluctant in helping me build family and family security.

WITH IT: My spouse and I are in one mind. Synchronized goal setting and accomplishing.

FOR COUPLE/GROUP:

Blood of Jesus Christ on our BEDS so that the Word of God can be Undefiled in our relationship/s.

Blood of Jesus Christ on my:

BELT OF TRUTH so that the Word of God can establish Spiritual Autonomy in my life.

REFERENCES:

1 JOHN 3:18-19. *Dear children, **let us not love with words or tongue but with actions and in truth.** This then is how we know that we belong to the truth, and how we set our hearts at rest in his presence*

2 COR 13:8-9. **For we cannot do anything against the truth**, *but only for the truth.*

JOHN 17:17. **Sanctify them by the truth**; *your word is truth.*

JOHN 16:13-14. *But when he, the Spirit of truth, comes, he will guide you into all truth. He will not speak on his own; **he will speak only what he hears, and he will tell you what is yet to come.***

JOHN 14:6. *Jesus answered, "I am the way and the truth and the life. **No one comes to the Father except through me.***

PROV 23:23. **Buy the truth and do not sell it**; *get wisdom, discipline and understanding.*

PSALMS 96:13. *they will sing before the LORD, for he comes, he comes to judge the earth. **He will judge the world in righteousness and the peoples in his truth.***

PHYSICAL ATTRIBUTE ADVANTAGES OF THE BELT OF TRUTH:
It states who I am in Christ.

WITHOUT IT: I wrestle with condemnation.

WITH IT: I state who I am in Christ to every word and thought contrary.

FOR COUPLE/GROUP:
Blood of Jesus Christ on our BELTS OF TRUTH so that the Word of God can establish Spiritual Autonomy in our relationship/s.

Blood of Jesus Christ on my:
BREASTPLATE OF RIGHTEOUSNESS so that the Word of God can establish a Treasure Auto Defense System in my life.

REFERENCES:

PSALMS 9:8. *He will judge the world in righteousness;* ***he will govern the peoples with justice.***

PSALMS 18:24. ***The LORD has rewarded me according to my righteousness,*** *according to the cleanness of my hands in his sight.*

PSALMS 33:5. ***The LORD loves righteousness and justice;*** *the earth is full of his unfailing love.*

PSALMS 36:6. ***Your righteousness is like the mighty mountains,*** *your justice like the great deep. O LORD, you preserve both man and beast.*

PSALMS 85:10. *Love and faithfulness meet together;* ***righteousness and peace kiss each other.***

PSALMS 85:13. ***Righteousness goes before him and prepares the way for his steps.***

PROV 13:6. ***Righteousness guards the man of integrity,*** *but wickedness overthrows the sinner.*

MATT 18:4. *Therefore,* ***whoever humbles himself like this child is the greatest in the kingdom of heaven.*** *"And whoever welcomes a little child like this in my name welcomes me.*

LUKE 12:33-34. *Sell your possessions and give to the poor. Provide purses for yourselves that will not wear out, a treasure in heaven that will not be exhausted, where no thief comes near and no moth destroys.* **For where your treasure is, there your heart will be also.**

1 TIM 6:17-19. *Command those who are rich in this present world not to be arrogant nor to put their hope in wealth, which is so uncertain, but to put their hope in God, who richly provides us with everything for our enjoyment.* **Command them to do good, to be rich in good deeds, and to be generous and willing to share. In this way they will lay up treasure for themselves as a firm foundation for the coming age,** *so that they may take hold of the life that is truly life.*

PHYSICAL ATTRIBUTE ADVANTAGES OF THE BREASTPLATE OF RIGHTEOUSNESS: Protects My Child Like Faith and other Spiritual Assets I've attained.

WITHOUT IT: I lean towards wanting to fight the fight myself.

WITH IT: I trust Christ as a Child trusts their parents.

FOR COUPLE/GROUP:

Blood of Jesus Christ on our BREASTPLATES OF RIGHTEOUSNESS so that the Word of God can establish a Treasure Auto Defense Systems in our relationship/s.

Blood of Jesus Christ on my:

SHIELD OF FAITH so that the Word of God can establish an Auto Spiritual Defense System in my life.

REFERENCES:

PROV 30:5. *"Every word of God is flawless; he is a shield to those who take refuge in him.*

PSALMS 28:7. **The LORD is my strength and my shield; my heart trusts in him,** *and I am helped. My heart leaps for joy and I will give thanks to him in song.*

PSALMS 5:12. *For surely, O LORD,* **you bless the righteous; you surround them with your favor as with a shield.**

PSALMS 3:3. *But you are a shield around me, O LORD; you bestow glory on me and lift up my head.*

ISAIAH 7:9. *The head of Ephraim is Samaria, and the head of Samaria is only Remaliah's son.* **If you do not stand firm in your faith, you will not stand at all.'"**

1 PET 1:4-6. **who through faith are shielded by God's power** *until the coming of the salvation that is ready to be revealed in the last time.*

HEB 11:33-34. **who through faith conquered kingdoms, administered justice, and gained what was promised; who shut the mouths of lions,**

2 COR 5:7. **We live by faith,** *not by sight.*

PHYSICAL ATTRIBUTE ADVANTAGES OF THE SHIELD OF FAITH: Auto Pilot Defense for Common Predictable Attacks.

WITHOUT IT: I'm hesitant about trusting auto pilot defense.

WITH IT: Anytime, Anywhere my shield is ready.

FOR COUPLE/GROUP:

Blood of Jesus Christ on our SHIELDS OF FAITH so that the Word of God can establish and Auto Spiritual Defense Systems in our relationship/s.

Blood of Jesus Christ on my:

HELMET OF SALVATION so that the Word of God can establish an Auto Thought Management System in my life.

REFERENCES:

ISAIAH 59:17. **He put on** *righteousness as his breastplate, and* **the helmet of salvation on his head;** *he put on the garments of vengeance and wrapped himself in zeal as in a cloak.*

ISAIAH 55:9. *"As the heavens are higher than the earth, so are* **my ways higher than your ways and my thoughts than your thoughts.**

PSALMS 13:2. **How long must I wrestle with my thoughts** *and every day have sorrow in my heart? How long will my enemy triumph over me?*

2 COR 10:5-6. **We demolish arguments and every pretension that sets itself up against the knowledge of God, and we take captive every thought to make it obedient to Christ.**

1 COR 1:10. *I appeal to you, brothers, in the name of our Lord Jesus Christ, that all of you agree with one another so that there may be no divisions among you and* **that you may be perfectly united in mind and thought.**

PHYSICAL ATTRIBUTE ADVANTAGES OF THE HELMET OF SALVATION: Neutralizes any lies that would other wise demand my attention.

WITHOUT IT: I spend a lot of my time consumed with sorting out which is the truth and which is a lie.

WITH IT: The more Word of God I know the less chaos I have inside my head.

FOR COUPLE/GROUP:
Blood of Jesus Christ on our HELMETS OF SALVATION so that the Word of God can establish Auto Thought Management Systems in our relationship/s.

Blood of Jesus Christ on my:
SWORD OF THE SPIRIT so that the Word of God can establish a Manual Spiritual Defense System in my life.

REFERENCES:

EPH 6:17. *Take the helmet of salvation and **the sword of the Spirit, which is the word of God**.*

HEB 4:12. ***For the word of God is living and active.*** *Sharper than any double-edged sword, it penetrates even to dividing soul and spirit, joints and marrow; it judges the thoughts and attitudes of the heart.*

HEB 6:5-6. ***who have tasted the goodness of the word of God and the powers of the coming age,***

2 COR 2:9-11. *If you forgive anyone, I also forgive him. And what I have forgiven- if there was anything to forgive-I have forgiven in the sight of Christ for your sake, **in order that Satan might not outwit us. For we are not unaware of his schemes.***

COL 4:5-6. ***Be wise in the way you act toward outsiders;*** *make the most of every opportunity. Let your conversation be always full of grace, seasoned with salt, so that you may know how to answer everyone.*

MATT 10:16. *I am sending you out like sheep among wolves. **Therefore be as shrewd as snakes and as innocent as doves.***

MATT 10:17-20. ***"Be on your guard against men;*** *they will hand you over to the local councils and flog you in their synagogues. On my account you will be brought before governors and kings as witnesses to them and to the Gentiles. But when they arrest you, **do not worry about what to say or how to say it. At that time you will be given what to say, for it will not be you speaking, but the Spirit of your Father speaking through you.***

PHYSICAL ATTRIBUTE ADVANTAGES OF THE SWORD OF THE SPIRIT: Manual Defense for uncommon attacks.

WITHOUT IT: I tend to be more talk then action.

WITH IT: I hunger for the front lines of the battle.

FOR COUPLE/GROUP:

Blood of Jesus Christ on our SWORDS OF THE SPIRIT so that the Word of God can establish Manual Spiritual Defense Systems in our relationship/s.

Blood of Jesus Christ on my:

STANCE so that the Word of God can establish a Physical Position in my life.

REFERENCES:

REV 6:17. *For the great day of their wrath has come, and **who can stand?"***

COL 4:12. *Epaphras, who is one of you and a servant of Christ Jesus, sends greetings. **He is always wrestling in prayer for you, that you may stand firm in all the will of God, mature and fully assured.***

EPH 6:13. *Therefore put on the full armor of God, **so that when the day of evil comes, you may be able to stand your ground,** and after you have done everything, to stand.*

1 COR 16:13-14. ***Be on your guard; stand firm in the faith;** be men of courage; be strong.*

1 COR 15:58. *Therefore, my dear brothers, stand firm. **Let nothing move you.***

LUKE 21:36. *Be always on the watch, and pray that you may be able to escape all that is about to happen, and **that you may be able to stand before the Son of Man."***

PROV 10:25. *When the storm has swept by, the wicked are gone, **but the righteous stand firm forever.***

PSALMS 33:11. *But **the plans of the LORD stand firm forever**, the purposes of his heart through all generations.*

MATT 13:18-23. *"Listen then to what the parable of the sower means: When anyone hears the message about the kingdom and does not understand it, the evil one comes and snatches away what was sown in his heart. This is the seed sown along the path. The one who received the seed that fell on rocky places is the man who hears the word and at once receives it with joy. But since he has no* root, he lasts only a short time. When trouble or persecution comes because of the word, he quickly falls away. The one who received the seed that fell among the thorns is the man who hears the word, but the worries of this life and the deceitfulness of wealth choke it, making it unfruitful. **But the one who received the seed that fell on good soil is the man who hears the word and understands it. He produces a crop, yielding a hundred, sixty or thirty times what was sown."**

DEUT 11:24-25. **Every place where you set your foot will be yours:** Your territory will extend from the desert to Lebanon, and from the Euphrates River to the western sea. No man will be able to stand against you. The LORD your God, as he promised you, will put the terror and fear of you on the whole land, wherever you go.

JOSH 1:3-4. **I will give you every place where you set your foot,** as I promised Moses.

PROV 4:27. **Do not swerve to the right or the left; keep your foot from evil.**

LUKE 21:19. **By standing firm you will gain life.**

PHYSICAL ATTRIBUTE ADVANTAGES OF THE STANCE: Testing point on How Well I'm Prepared.

WITHOUT IT: I'm more worried about how observers think I look versus the spiritual impact my performance will have.

WITH IT: I test worse case scenarios until I'm confident.

FOR COUPLE/GROUP:

Blood of Jesus Christ on our STANCES so that the Word of God can establish Physical Positions in our relationship/s.

<u>Blood of Jesus Christ on my:</u>

WARRIOR'S MIND FRAME so that the Word of God can establish Prayer with God and for the Saints in my life.

REFERENCES:

PROV 15:8. The LORD detests the sacrifice of the wicked, but the **prayer of the upright pleases him.**

PROV 15:29. The LORD is far from the wicked but **he hears the prayer of the righteous.**

JOHN 17:18. **Sanctify them by the truth;** your word is truth.

COL. 4:12-13. *Epaphras, who is one of you and a servant of Christ Jesus, sends greetings.* **He is always wrestling in prayer for you, that you may stand firm in all the will of God, mature and fully assured.**

1 PET 3:10-12. *For, "Whoever would love life and see good days must keep his tongue from evil and his lips from deceitful speech. He must turn from evil and do good; he must seek peace and pursue it.* **For the eyes of the Lord are on the righteous and his ears are attentive to their prayer,**

JOHN 17:13-23. *"...I have given them your word and the world has hated them, for they are not of the world any more than I am of the world.* **My prayer is not that you take them out of the world but that you protect them from the evil one.** *They are not of the world, even as I am not of it. Sanctify them by the truth; your word is truth. As you sent me into the world, I have sent them into the world. For them I sanctify myself, that they too may be truly sanctified. "My prayer is not for them alone. I pray also for those who will believe in me through their message, that all of them may be one, Father, just as you are in me and I am in you. May they also be in us so that the world may believe that you have sent me. I have given them the glory that you gave me, that they may be one as we are one: I in them and you in me. May they be brought to complete unity to let the world know that you sent me and have loved them even as you have loved me.*

LEV 18:28. **And if you defile the land, it will vomit you out** *as it vomited out the nations that were before you.*

PROV 2:21-22. **For the upright will live in the land, and the blameless will remain in it; but the wicked will be cut off from the land, and the unfaithful will be torn from it.**

COL 1:4-5. *because we have heard of* **your** *faith in Christ Jesus and of the* **love you have for all the saints-**

EPH 6:18. *And pray in the Spirit on all occasions with all kinds of prayers and requests. With this in mind, be alert* **and always keep on praying for all the saints.**

ROM 8:27. *And he who searches our hearts knows the mind of the Spirit, because the* **Spirit intercedes for the saints in accordance with God's will.**

DAN 7:17-18. **But the saints of the Most High will receive the kingdom and will** *possess it forever-yes, for ever and ever.'*

PHYSICAL ATTRIBUTE ADVANTAGES OF THE WARRIOR'S MIND FRAME: Encrypted Spiritual Communication only the Holy Spirit can Decipher. Value of Team covering each others blind spots and back sides.

WITHOUT IT: I lean towards trusting the physical more than the spiritual. I feel more confident in myself than my team.

WITH IT: Addicted to living life by faith versus sight. The value of team out weights my personal opinions.

FOR COUPLE/GROUP:

Blood of Jesus Christ on our WARRIOR'S MIND FRAMES so that the Word of God can establish Prayer with God and for the Saints in our relationship/s.

Blood of Jesus Christ on my:

FAITH so that the Word of God can Move Mountains in my life.

REFERENCES:

HEB 11:1. **Now faith is the substance of things hoped for, the evidence of things not seen.** KJV

JAMES 2:26. *For as the body without the spirit is dead,* **so faith without works is dead also.** KJV

HEB 11:6. *And* **without faith it is impossible to please God,** *because anyone who comes to him must believe that he exists and that he rewards those who earnestly seek him.*

HEB 12:2-3. *Let* **us fix our eyes on Jesus, the author and perfecter of our faith,** *who for the joy set before him endured the cross, scorning its shame, and sat down at the right hand of the throne of God.*

GAL 3:6-7. *Consider Abraham:* **"He believed God, and it was credited to him as righteousness."**

MATT 17:20. *He replied, "Because you have so little faith. I tell you the truth,* **if you have faith as small as a mustard seed, you can say to this mountain, 'Move from here to there' and it will move.** *Nothing will be impossible for you."*

PHYSICAL ATTRIBUTE ADVANTAGES OF FAITH: Unlimited: Creativity, Strength and Elasticity.

WITHOUT IT: Limited Options. I lean towards rationalizing how things work and how they will turn out. It's hard to visualize.

WITH IT: I embrace with all five senses, more the eternal entities than the temporary fading entities.

FOR COUPLE/GROUP:

Blood of Jesus Christ on our FAITH so that the Word of God can Move Mountians in our relationship/s.

Blood of Jesus Christ on my:

HOPE so that the Word of God can Manifest Restoration in my life.

REFERENCES:

JOB 13:15-16. *Though he slay me, yet will I hope in him; I will surely defend my ways to his face.* Indeed, this will turn out for my deliverance, for no godless man would dare come before him!

JOB 14:19. *as water wears away stones and torrents wash away the soil, so you destroy man's hope.*

PSALM 9:18. But the needy will not always be forgotten, *nor the hope of the afflicted ever perish.*

PSALM 33:18-19. But *the eyes of the LORD are* on those who fear him, *on those whose hope is in his unfailing love, to deliver them from death and keep them alive in famine.*

PSALM 37:9. For evil men will be cut off, but *those who hope in the LORD will inherit the land.*

PSALM 119:43. *Do not snatch the word of truth from my mouth, for I have put my hope in your laws.*

PSALM 119:74. May those who fear you rejoice when they see me, *for I have put my hope in your word.*

PROV 13:12. *Hope deferred makes the heart sick, but a longing fulfilled is a tree of life.*

PROV 23:18. There is surely a future hope for you, and *your hope will not be cut off.*

ISA 40:31. *but those who hope in the LORD will renew their strength.*

HOS 2:15. *There I will give her back her vineyards, and will make the Valley of Achor a door of hope.* There she will sing as in the days of her youth, as in the day she came up out of Egypt.

ROM 8:24-25. *For in this hope we were saved.* But hope that is seen is no hope at all. Who hopes for what he already has? But if we hope for what we do not yet have, we wait for it patiently.

ROM 15:13. *May the God of hope fill you with all joy and peace as you trust in him, so that you may overflow with hope by the power of the Holy Spirit.*

COL. 1:4-7. *the faith and love that spring from the hope that is stored up for you in heaven and that you have already heard about in the word of truth,* the gospel that has come to you. All over the world this gospel is bearing fruit and growing, just as it has been doing among you since the day you heard it and understood God's grace in all its truth.

1 THESS 4:13-14. *Brothers, we do not want you* to be ignorant about those who fall asleep, or *to grieve like the rest of men, who have no hope.*

1 THESS 5:7-8. But since we belong to the day, let us be self-controlled, putting on faith and love as a breastplate, and *the hope of salvation as a helmet.*

1 TIM 6:17-18. Command those who are rich in this present world not to be arrogant nor to put their hope in wealth, which is so uncertain, *but to put their hope in God, who richly provides us with everything for our enjoyment.*

HEB 6:19. *We have this hope as an anchor for the soul, firm and secure.* It enters the inner sanctuary behind the curtain,

1 JOHN 3:3. *Everyone who has this hope in him purifies himself,* just as he is pure.

PHYSICAL ATTRIBUTE ADVANTAGES OF HOPE: Exponential Motivation Enhancer.

WITHOUT IT: I lack the desire to press on when the stress is on.

WITH IT: My desire produces life, protects me and renews me.

FOR COUPLE/GROUP:
Blood of Jesus Christ on our HOPE so that the Word of God can Manifest Restoration in our relationship/s.

Blood of Jesus Christ on my:
LOVE so that the Word of God can Dismantle All of the Fears in my life.

REFERENCES:

PSALM 26:3 for *your love is ever before me*, and I walk continually in your truth.

1 COR 13:4-13 *Love is patient, love is kind.* It does not envy, it does not boast, it is not proud. It is not rude, it is not self-seeking, it is not easily angered, it keeps no record of wrongs. *Love does not delight in evil but rejoices with the truth.* It always protects, always trusts, always hopes, always perseveres. *Love never fails.* But where there are prophecies, they will cease; where there

are tongues, they will be stilled; where there is knowledge, it will pass away. For we know in part and we prophesy in part, but when perfection comes, the imperfect disappears. When I was a child, I talked like a child, I thought like a child, I reasoned like a child. When I became a man, I put childish ways behind me. Now we see but a poor reflection as in a mirror; then we shall see face to face. Now I know in part; then I shall know fully, even as I am fully known. **And now these three remain: faith, hope and love. But the greatest of these is love.**

1 JOHN 4:12 *No one has ever seen God;* **but if we love one another,** *God lives in us and **his love is made complete in us**.*

ROM 13:10 **Love worketh no ill** *to his neighbour:* **therefore love is the fulfilling of the law. KJV**

1 JOHN 4:18 **There is no fear in love. But perfect love drives out fear,** *because fear has to do with punishment.* **The one who fears is not made perfect in love.**

PROV18:21 **The tongue has the power of life and death, and those who love it will eat its fruit.**

PROV 17:9 **He who covers over an offense promotes love,** *but whoever repeats the matter separates close friends.*

PROV 20:28 **Love and faithfulness keep a king safe; through love his throne is made secure.**

PROV 21:21 **He who pursues** *righteousness and* **love finds life, prosperity and honor.**

MATT 5:45-47 **If you love those who love you, what reward will you get?** *Are not even the tax collectors doing that?*

1 PETER 4:8-9 *Above all,* **love each other deeply, because love covers over a multitude of sins.** *Offer hospitality to one another without grumbling.*

PHYSICAL ATTRIBUTE ADVANTAGES OF LOVE: Infinite Dimensions with Infinite Senses.

WITHOUT IT: I tend to hide. Run from protection.

WITH IT: I have an appetite for unlocking physical, emotional and spiritual mysteries.

FOR COUPLE/GROUP:

Blood of Jesus Christ on our LOVE so that the Word of God can Dismantle All of the Fears in our relationship/s.

Blood of Jesus Christ on my:

HONOR so that the Word of God can be Glorified in my life.

REFERENCES:

1 PETER 2:17 *Show **proper respect to everyone:** Love the brotherhood of believers, fear God, **honor the king.***

2 PETER 1:17-18 ***For he received honor and glory** from God the Father **when the voice came to him from the Majestic Glory,** saying, "This is my Son, whom I love; with him I am well pleased." We ourselves heard this voice that came from heaven when we were with him on the sacred mountain.*

REV 4:11 ***"You are worthy,** our Lord and God, **to receive** glory and **honor** and power, **for you created all things, and by your will** they were created and have their being."*

1 PETER 1:7-8 *These have come so that **your faith-of greater worth than gold,** which perishes even though **refined by fire**-may be proved genuine and **may result in** praise, glory and **honor** when Jesus Christ is revealed.*

HEB 3:3-4 ***Jesus has been found worthy of greater honor than Moses, just as the builder of a house has greater honor than the house itself.***

HEB 2:9 *But **we see Jesus, who was made a little lower than the angels, now crowned with** glory and **honor because he suffered death,** so that by the grace of God he might taste death for everyone.*

ROM 13:7 *Give everyone what you owe him: If you owe taxes, pay taxes; if revenue, then revenue; if respect, then respect; **if honor, then honor.***

ROM 12:10-11 *Be devoted to one another in brotherly love. **Honor one another above yourselves.***

ACTS 7:41-42 *That was the time they made an idol in the form of a calf. They brought sacrifices to it and **held a celebration in honor of what their hands had made.***

JOHN 12:26 *Whoever serves me must follow me; and where I am, my servant also will be. **My Father will honor the one who serves me.***

JOHN 7:18 *He who speaks on his own does so to gain honor for himself, **but he who works for the honor of the one who sent him is a man of truth; there is nothing false about him.***

JOHN 5:23 *that **all may honor the Son just as they honor the Father. He who does not honor the Son does not honor the Father, who sent him.***

MATT 15:8 ***"'These people honor me with their lips,** but their hearts are far from me.*

117

ZEPH 3:19-20 *At that time I will deal with all who oppressed you; I will rescue the lame and gather those who have been scattered.* **I will give them praise and honor in every land where they were put to shame.** *At that time I will gather you; at that time I will bring you home.* **I will give you honor and praise among all the peoples of the earth when I restore your fortunes before your very eyes,"** *says the LORD.*

PROV 18:12 *Before his downfall a man's heart is proud,* **but humility comes before honor.**

PROV 20:3 **It is to a man's honor to avoid strife,** *but every fool is quick to quarrel.*

PROV 3:35 **The wise inherit honor,** *but fools he holds up to shame.*

PROV 4:8 *Esteem her, and she will exalt you;* **embrace her, and she will honor you.**

PHYSICAL ATTRIBUTE ADVANTAGES OF HONOR: A Set of Choices that Produces Celebration.

WITHOUT IT: Habitual cycles of incomplete closures. Desperate for praise.

WITH IT: Enjoyable work ethics. Accomplishments gratifying.

FOR COUPLE/GROUP:
Blood of Jesus Christ on our HONOR so that the Word of God can be Glorified in our relationship/s.

Blood of Jesus Christ on my:
INTEGRITY so that the Word of God can be Steadfast in my life.

REFERENCES:

DEUT 9:4-5 **It is not because of** *your righteousness or* **your integrity that you are going in to take possession of their land;** *but on account of the wickedness of these nations, the LORD your God will drive them out before you, to accomplish what he swore to your fathers, to Abraham, Isaac and Jacob.*

NEH 7:2-3 **I put in charge of Jerusalem** *my brother Hanani, along with Hananiah the commander of the citadel,* **because he was a man of integrity** *and feared God more than most men do.*

JOB 2:9 *His wife said to him, "Are you still holding on to your integrity? Curse God and die!"*

PSALM 7:8 *let the LORD judge the peoples. **Judge me, O LORD,** according to my righteousness, **according to my integrity, O Most High.***

PSALM 25:21 ***May integrity** and uprightness **protect me, because my hope is in you.***

PSALM 41:12 ***In my integrity you uphold me and set me in your presence forever.***

PSALM 78:72 *And **David shepherded them with integrity of heart;** with skillful hands he led them.*

PROV 10:9 ***The man of integrity walks securely,** but he who takes crooked paths will be found out.*

PROV 11:3 ***The integrity of the upright guides them,** but the unfaithful are destroyed by their duplicity.*

PROV 13:6 ***Righteousness guards the man of integrity,** but wickedness overthrows the sinner.*

PROV 17:26 ***It is not good** to punish an innocent man, or **to flog officials for their integrity.***

ISIAHA *45:23 By **myself I have sworn, my mouth has uttered in all integrity a word that will not be revoked:** Before me every knee will bow; by me every tongue will swear.*

PHYSICAL ATTRIBUTE ADVANTAGES OF INTEGRITY: A Set of Choices that Persistently Produces a Standard.

WITHOUT IT: Right and wrong have no value. I lean towards only doing what profits me. I'm always right.

WITH IT: People and organizations seek my council. I'm respected and admired.

FOR COUPLE/GROUP:

Blood of Jesus Christ on our INTEGRITY so that the Word of God can be Steadfast in our relationship/s.

Blood of Jesus Christ on my:

SKILLS so that the Word of God can Protect My Safe Haven in my life.

REFERENCES:

DEUT 33:11 **Bless all his skills, O LORD, and be pleased with the work of his hands.** *Smite the loins of those who rise up against him; strike his foes till they rise no more."*

EXO 35:31-35 **and he has filled him with the Spirit of God, with skill, ability and knowledge in all kinds of crafts —** *to make artistic designs for work in gold, silver and bronze, to cut and set stones, to work in wood and to engage in all kinds of artistic craftsmanship. And he has given both him and Oholiab son of Ahisamach, of the tribe of Dan, the ability to teach others. He has filled them with skill to do all kinds of work as craftsmen, designers, embroiderers in blue, purple and scarlet yarn and fine linen, and weavers —* **all of them master craftsmen and designers.**

EXO 36:1 *So Bezalel, Oholiab and* **every skilled person to whom the LORD has given skill and ability to know how to carry out all the work of constructing** *the sanctuary are to do the work just as the LORD has commanded."*

ECCL 2:19-22 *And who knows whether he will be a wise man or a fool? Yet* **he will have control over all the work into which I have poured my effort and skill under the sun.** *This too is meaningless. So my heart began to despair over all my*

toilsome labor under the sun. For a **man may do his work with wisdom, knowledge and skill, and then he must leave all he owns to someone who has not worked for it.** *This too is meaningless and a great misfortune.*

ECCL 10:10 **If the ax is dull and its edge unsharpened,** *more strength is needed but* **skill will bring success.**

EZEK 28:5 **By your great skill in trading you have increased your wealth**, and *because of your wealth your heart has grown proud.*

PHYSICAL ATTRIBUTE ADVANTAGES OF SKILLS: A Set of Tasks that Produces a Valued Tangible/Intangible Asset.

WITHOUT IT: Dependent. Temporary fixes. I tend to act like I know what I'm talking about when I don't.

WITH IT: Independent. Minimal, jack of all traits. Resourceful.

FOR COUPLE/GROUP:

Blood of Jesus Christ on our SKILLS so that the Word of God can Protect Our Safe Havens in our relationship/s.

Blood of Jesus Christ on my:
FINANCES so that the Word of God can Create My Safe Haven in my life.

REFERENCES:

1 PETER 5:2-4 *Be shepherds* of God's flock that is under your care, serving as overseers-not because you must, but because you are willing, as God wants you to be; *not greedy for money, but eager to serve*; not lording it over those entrusted to you, but being examples to the flock. And when the Chief Shepherd appears, *you will receive the crown of glory that will never fade away.*

JAMES 4:13-15 Now listen, *you who say, "Today or tomorrow we will go to this or that city, spend a year there, carry on business and make money."* Why, you do not even know what will happen tomorrow. What is your life? You are a mist that appears for a little while and then vanishes. Instead, *you ought to say, "If it is the Lord's will, we will live and do this or that."*

HEB 13:4-5 *Keep your lives free from the love of money and be content with what you have,* because God has said, "Never will I leave you; never will I forsake you."

1 TIM 6:10 *For the love of money is a root of all kinds of evil.* Some people, eager for money, have wandered from the faith and pierced themselves with many grief's.

ACTS 8:20-21 Peter answered: *"May your money perish with you, because you thought you could buy the gift of God with money!*

ISAIAH 55:2 *Why spend money on what is not bread, and your labor on what does not satisfy? Listen, listen to me, and eat what is good, and your soul will delight in the richest of fare.*

ISAIAH 55:1 "Come, all you who are thirsty, come to the waters; and *you who have no money, come, buy and eat! Come, buy wine and milk without money and without cost.*

ECCL 10:19 A feast is made for laughter, and wine makes life merry, but *money is the answer for everything.*

PROV 17:16 *Of what use is money in the hand of a fool,* since he has no desire to get wisdom?

PROV 13:11 Dishonest money dwindles away, but *he who gathers money little by little makes it grow.*

PSALM 15:5 *who lends his money without usury and does not accept a bribe against the innocent. He who does these things will never be shaken.*

NEH 10-11 I and my brothers and my *men are also lending the people money and grain. But let the exacting of usury stop!* Give back to them immediately their fields, vineyards, olive groves and houses, and also the usury you are charging them-the hundredth part of the money, grain, new wine and oil."

EXO 22:25-26 *"If you lend money to one of my people among you who is needy, do not be like a moneylender; charge him no interest.*

ECCL 7:12 **Wisdom is a shelter as money is a shelter,** but the advantage of knowledge is this: that wisdom preserves the life of its possessor.

ECCL 5:10 **Whoever loves money never has money enough; whoever loves wealth is never satisfied with his income.** This too is meaningless.

PHYSICAL ATTRIBUTE ADVANTAGES OF FINANCES: A Set of Expenses Accountable to a Set of Incomes.

WITHOUT IT: My relationships tend to be stressed. Quenchless. Socialistic views.

WITH IT: Entrepreneurial. Contented. Prepared.

FOR COUPLE/GROUP:
Blood of Jesus Christ on our FINANCES so that the Word of God can Create Our Safe Havens in our relationship/s.

Blood of Jesus Christ on my:
INCOME PRODUCING ENTITIES so that the Word of God can Reveal Creations Hidden Mysteries in my life.

REFERENCES:

PSALMS 1:3 **He is like a tree planted by streams of water,** which yields its fruit in season and whose leaf does not wither. **Whatever he does prospers.**

PROV 15:6 The house of the righteous contains great treasure, but **the income of the wicked brings them trouble.**

JER 33:3 **'Call to me and I will answer you and tell you great and unsearchable things you do not know.'**

PROV 31:16 **She considers a field and buys it; out of her earnings she plants a vineyard.**

MATT 25:14-27 "Again, it will be like a man going on a journey, who called his servants and entrusted his property to them. To one he gave five talents of money, to another two talents, and to another one talent, each according to his ability. Then he went on his journey. **The man who had received the five talents** went at once **and put his money to work and gained five more.** So also, **the one with the two talents gained two more.** But the man who had received the one talent went off, dug a hole in the ground and hid his master's money. "After a long time the master of those servants returned and settled accounts *with them. The man who had received the five talents brought the other five. 'Master,' he said,* **'you entrusted me with five talents. See, I have gained five more.'** *"His master replied, 'Well done, good and faithful servant!* **You have been faithful with a few things; I will put you in charge of many things.** *Come and share your master's happiness!' "The man with the two talents also came. 'Master,' he said,* **'you entrusted me with two talents; see, I have gained two more.'** *"His master replied,* **'Well done, good and faithful servant! You have been faithful with a few things; I will put you in charge of many things.**

LEV 26:3-5 **"If you follow my ways, I will send you rain in its season, and the ground will yield its crops and the trees of the field their fruit.** *Your threshing will continue until grape harvest and the grape harvest will continue until planting, and* **you will eat all the food you want** *and live in safety in your land.*

PROV 8:19 **Wisdom - My fruit is better than fine gold; what I yield surpasses choice silver.**

EZEK 34:27-28 **The trees of the field will yield their fruit and the ground will yield its crops;** *the people will be secure in their land. They will know that I am the LORD,* **when I break the bars of their yoke and rescue them from the hands of those who enslaved them.**

PHYSICAL ATTRIBUTE ADVANTAGES OF INCOME PRODUCING ENTITIES: A Set of Expenses less than a Set of Incomes for Oneself.

WITHOUT IT: Stagnation. Ineffective leadership and managerial skills.

WITH IT: Self-sustaining. Supports additional families. Cost effective solutions.

FOR COUPLE/GROUP:
Blood of Jesus Christ on our INCOME PRODUCING ENTITIES so that the Word of God can Reveal Creations Hidden Mysteries in our relationship/s.

Blood of Jesus Christ on my:
NON-PROFIT ENTITIES so that the Word of God can Reveal the Hidden Mysteries in my life.

REFERENCES:
JER 33:3 **'Call to me and I will answer you and tell you great and unsearchable things you do not know.'**

PROV 20:5 *The purposes of a man's heart are deep waters,* but *a man of understanding draws them out.*

DEUT 10:18-19 *He defends the cause of the fatherless and the widow, and loves the alien, giving him food and clothing.*

DEUT 15:7-8 *If there is a poor man among your brothers in any of the towns* of the land that the *LORD your God is giving you, do not be hardhearted or tightfisted toward your poor brother.*

DEUT 28:8 *The LORD will send a blessing on your barns and on everything you put your hand to.* The LORD your God will bless you *in the land he is giving you.*

JUDG 2:23 The LORD had allowed those nations to remain; *he did not drive them out at once by giving them into the hands of Joshua.*

PROV 15:23 *A man finds joy in giving an apt reply* – and how good is a timely word!

2 COR 8:7 But just as you excel in everything-in faith, in speech, in knowledge, in complete earnestness and in your love for us - *see that you also excel in this grace of giving.*

COL 3:17 And *whatever you do, whether in word or deed, do it all* in the name of the Lord Jesus, *giving thanks to God* the Father through him.

PHYSICAL ATTRIBUTE ADVANTAGES OF NON-PROFIT ENTITES:
A Set of Expenses less than a Set of Incomes Shared by Others.

WITHOUT IT: Lacks ingenuity to meet community's needs. Invest more into presentation versus producing fruitful ministry.

WITH IT: Effectively sets community free from it's limitations. Bridge builder between resource centers.

FOR COUPLE/GROUP:
Blood of Jesus Christ on our NON-PROFIT ENTITIES so that the Word of God can Reveal the Hidden Mysteries in our relationship/s.

Blood of Jesus Christ on my:
HOME so that the Word of God can be a Safe Haven in my life.

REFERENCES:

2 SAM 7:10-11 And **I will provide a place for my people** Israel **and will plant them so that they can have a home of their own and no longer be disturbed.** Wicked people will not oppress them anymore, as they did at the beginning and have done ever since the time I appointed leaders over my people Israel. I will also give you rest from all your enemies.

1 CHRON 16:43 Then **all the people left, each for his own home,** and David returned home **to bless his family.**

PROV 15:31 **He who listens to a life-giving rebuke will be at home among the wise.**

DAN 6:10-11 Now when **Daniel learned that the decree had been published, he went home** to his upstairs room where the windows opened toward Jerusalem. Three times a day he got down on his knees and prayed, **giving thanks to his God, just as he had done before.**

ZEPH 3:20 At that time I will gather you; at that time **I will bring you home. I will give you honor and praise among all the peoples of the earth** when **I restore your fortunes before your very eyes," says the LORD.**

LUKE 8:39 **"Return home and tell how much God has done for you."** So the man went away and told all over town how much Jesus had done for him.

JOHN 14:23-24 Jesus replied, **"If anyone loves me,** he will obey my teaching. My Father will love him, and **we will come to him and make our home with him.**

PHILEM 1-2 to Apphia our sister, to Archippus our fellow soldier and **to the church that meets in your home:**

2 PETER 3:13 But in keeping with his promise **we are looking forward to a new heaven and a new earth, the home of righteousness.**

PHYSICAL ATTRIBUTE ADVANTAGES OF HOME: Security. Hope. Rest.

WITHOUT IT: Restless. I lean towards expecting people to comply to my personal needs.

WITH IT: Artesian well of sanity, comfort and celebration.

FOR COUPLE/GROUP:

Blood of Jesus Christ on our HOME so that the Word of God can be a Safe Haven in our relationship/s.

Blood of Jesus Christ on my:

ASSETS so that the Word of God can be a Store House in my life.

REFERENCES:

GEN 13:5-7 *Now Lot, who was moving about with Abram, also had flocks and herds and tents. But the land could not support them while they stayed together, **for their possessions were so great that they were not able to stay together.** And quarreling arose between Abram's herdsmen and the herdsmen of Lot. The Canaanites and Perizzites were also living in the land at that time.*

DEUT 28:12 **The LORD will open the heavens, the storehouse of his bounty, to send rain on your land in season and to bless all the work of your hands.** *You will lend to many nations but will borrow from none.*

PROV 12:27 *The lazy man does not roast his game, but **the diligent man prizes his possessions.***

MATT 24:45-48 **"Who then is the faithful and wise servant, whom the master has put in charge of the servants in his household to give them their food at the proper time?** *It will be good for that servant whose master finds him doing so when he returns. I tell you the truth, **he will put him in charge of all his possessions.***

UKE 12:33-34 *Sell your possessions and give to the poor. Provide purses for yourselves that will not wear out, a treasure in heaven that will not be exhausted, where no thief comes near and no moth destroys. **For where your treasure is, there your heart will be also.***

2 COR 12:14-15 *Now I am ready to visit you for the third time, and I will not be a burden to you, **because what I want is not your possessions but you.** After all, children should not have to save up for their parents, but parents for their children.*

1 JOHN 3:17-19 **If anyone has material possessions and sees his brother in need but has no pity on him, how can the love of God be in him?** *Dear children, let us not love with words or tongue but with actions and in truth.*

PHYSICAL ATTRIBUTE ADVANTAGES OF ASSETS: Harnessed Resources for Multiplying.

WITHOUT IT: Drains ones spiritual, health and passion. Becomes a wall between my relationships.

WITH IT: Perpetuates. It becomes the fuel that drives my passion. It invigorates my desires to bless others.

FOR COUPLE/GROUP:

Blood of Jesus Christ on our ASSETS so that the Word of God can be a Store House in our relationship/s.

Blood of Jesus Christ on my:

LIABILITIES so that the Word of God can Quench My Thirst in my life.

REFERENCES:

DEUT 15:9-11 **Be careful not to harbor this wicked thought: "The seventh year, the year for canceling debts, is near," so that you do not show ill will toward your needy brother and give him nothing.** He may then appeal to the LORD against you, and you will be found guilty of sin. Give generously to him and do so without a grudging heart; then because of this the LORD your God will bless you in all your work and in everything you put your hand to. There will always be poor people in the land. Therefore I command you to be openhanded toward your brothers and toward the poor and needy in your land.

2 KINGS 4:7 She went and told the man of God, and he said, **"Go, sell the oil and pay your debts. You and your sons can live on what is left."**

PROV 22:26 **Do not be a man who strikes hands in pledge or puts up security for debts;**

JER 17:8 **He will be like a tree planted by the water that sends out its roots by the stream. It does not fear when heat comes; its leaves are always green. It has no worries in a year of drought and never fails to bear fruit."**

NIV MATT 6:12 **Forgive us our debts, as we also have forgiven our debtors.**

LUKE 7:42 **Neither of them had the money to pay him back, so he canceled the debts of both.** Now which of them will love him more?"

JOSH 6:18-19 But **keep away from the devoted things, so that you will not bring about your own destruction** by taking any of them. Otherwise you will make

the camp of Israel liable to destruction and bring trouble on it. All the silver and gold and the articles of bronze and iron are sacred to the LORD and must go into his treasury."

REV 7:16 **Never again will they hunger; never again will they thirst. The sun will not beat upon them, nor any scorching heat.**

PHYSICAL ATTRIBUTE ADVANTAGES OF LIBILITIES: Harnessed Resources for Dividing.

WITHOUT IT: I tend to justify going into debt. Limits future options.

WITH IT: Strengthens my integrity. Fixated on long term positive strategies.

FOR COUPLE/GROUP:
Blood of Jesus Christ on our LIBILITIES so that the Word of God can Quench Our Thirst in our relationship/s.

Blood of Jesus Christ on my:
MARRIAGE so that the Word of God can Comfort Me in the Night Hours in my life.

REFERENCES:
GEN 2:18 *The LORD God said, **"It is not good for the man to be alone. I will make a helper suitable for him."***

ECCL 4:11 *Also, **if two lie down together, they will keep warm.** But how can one keep warm alone?*

ECCL 4:12 *Though one may be overpowered, **two can defend themselves.** A cord of three strands is not quickly broken.*

JER 29:6-7 *Marry and have sons and daughters; **find wives for your sons and give your daughters in marriage, so that they too may have sons and daughters. Increase in number there;** do not decrease.*

DAN 11:17-18 *He will determine to come with the might of his entire kingdom and will make an alliance with the king of the South. **And he will give him a daughter in marriage in order to overthrow the kingdom, but his plans will not succeed or help him.***

MAL 2:14 ***You ask, "Why?" It is because the LORD is acting as the witness between you and the wife** of your youth, because you have broken faith with her, though she is your partner, the wife **of your marriage covenant.***

LUKE 2:36-38 *There was also a prophetess, Anna, the daughter of Phanuel, of the tribe of Asher. She was very old; she had lived with her husband seven years **after her marriage**, and then was a widow until she was eighty-four. **She never left the temple but worshiped night and day, fasting and praying.***

HEB 13:4-5 ***Marriage should be honored by all, and the marriage bed kept pure,** for God will judge the adulterer and all the sexually immoral.*

PHYSICAL ATTRIBUTE ADVANTAGES OF MARRIAGE: The Willingness to Continually Share of Oneself Physically, Emotionally and Spiritually with Another Intimately.

WITHOUT IT: I connect with sources that provide incomplete comfort. Loneliness creeps in.

WITH IT: Manifestations of surreal intimacy that transcends life experiences.

FOR COUPLE/GROUP:

Blood of Jesus Christ on our MARRIAGE so that the Word of God can Comfort Us in the Night Hours in our relationship/s.

Blood of Jesus Christ on my:

CHILDREN so that the Word of God can Establish My Legacy in my life.

REFERENCES:

GEN 3:16 *To the woman he said, "I will greatly increase your pains in childbearing;* **with pain you will give birth to children.** *Your desire will be for your husband, and he will rule over you."*

JOB 5:25 **You will know that your children will be many, and your descendants like the grass of the earth.**

PSALM 72:4 **He will defend** *the afflicted among the people* **and save the children of the needy;** *he will crush the oppressor.*

PSALM 78:4 **We will not hide them from their children; we will tell** *the next generation* **the praiseworthy deeds of the LORD, his power, and the wonders he has done.**

PSALM 112:2 **His children will be mighty in the land;** *the generation of the upright will be blessed.*

PSALM 127:3 **Sons are a heritage from the LORD, children a reward from him.**

PROV 13:22 **A good man leaves an inheritance for his children's children,** *but a sinner's wealth is stored up for the righteous.*

PROV 17:6 **Children's children are a crown to the aged,** *and parents are the pride of their children.*

ISAIAH 3:4 **I will make** *boys their officials; mere* **children** *will* **govern them.**

ISAIAH 49:20 **The children born during your bereavement will yet say** *in your hearing,* **'This place is too small for us; give us more space to live in.'**

HOS 11:10 *They will follow the LORD; he will roar like a lion. When he roars,* **his children will come trembling from the west.**

MAL 4:6 *He will turn the hearts of the fathers to their children, and the hearts of the children to their fathers;* or else I will come and strike the land with a curse."

MATT 11:25-26 At that time Jesus said, *"I praise you, Father, Lord of heaven and earth, because you have hidden these things from the wise and learned, and revealed them to little children.* Yes, Father, for this was your good pleasure.

MATT 19:14-15 Jesus said, *"Let the little children come to me, and do not hinder them, for the kingdom of heaven belongs to such as these."*

EPH 6:4 *Fathers, do not exasperate your children;* instead, bring them up in the training and instruction of the Lord.

COL 3:20-21 *Children, obey your parents in everything,* for this pleases the Lord. *Fathers, do not embitter your children,* or they will become discouraged.

PHYSICAL ATTRIBUTE ADVANTAGES OF CHILDREN: Multiplies Relationship Perception Options.

WITHOUT IT: My selfishness is exposed.

WITH IT: I discover intangible resource tools; love, forgiveness, faith, etc to enhance my life experience.

FOR COUPLE/GROUP:
Blood of Jesus Christ on our CHILDREN so that the Word of God can Establish Our Legacies in our relationship/s.

Blood of Jesus Christ on my:
FAMILY so that the Word of God can Produce and Guide My Offspring in my life.

REFERENCES:

NUM 1:4-5 One man from each tribe, each the *head of his family, is to help you.*

JOSH 2:12-13 Now then, *please swear to me* by the LORD that you *will show kindness to my family, because I have shown kindness to you.* Give me a sure sign that you will spare the lives of my father and mother, my brothers and sisters, and all who belong to them, and that you will save us from death."

JUDG 6:15 "But Lord," Gideon asked, "how can I save Israel? My clan is the weakest in Manasseh, and *I am the least in my family."*

1 CHRON 16:43 *Then all the people left, each for his own home, and **David returned home to bless his family.***

PROV 11:29 ***He who brings trouble on his family will inherit only wind**, and the fool will be servant to the wise.*

PROV 31:15 *She gets up while it is still dark; **she provides food for her family** and portions for her servant girls.*

ISAIAH 22:24 ***All the glory of his family will hang on him:** its offspring and offshoots — all its lesser vessels, from the bowls to all the jars.*

MARK 5:190 *Jesus did not let him, but said, **"Go home to your family and tell them how much the Lord has done for you**, and how he has had mercy on you."*

JOHN 8:34-36 *Jesus replied, "I tell you the truth, everyone who sins is a slave to sin. **Now a slave has no permanent place in the family, but a son belongs to it forever.***

1 TIM 3:4-6 ***He must manage his own family well** and see that his children obey him with proper respect. If anyone does not know how to manage his own family, how can he take care of God's church?*

1 TIM 5:8 ***If anyone does not provide for his relatives, and especially for his immediate family, he has denied the faith and is worse than an unbeliever.***

PHYSICAL ATTRIBUTE ADVANTAGES OF FAMILY: Multiplies Networking Perception Options.

WITHOUT IT: I rely on intimidation to cover up my lack of good parenting skills.

WITH IT: I develop multiple ways on how to communicate patience, comfort and companionship.

FOR COUPLE/GROUP:
Blood of Jesus Christ on our FAMILY so that the Word of God can Produce and Guide Our Offspring in our relationship/s.

Blood of Jesus Christ on my:
FRIENDS so that the Word of God can Create Faithful Companions in my life.

REFERENCES:
JOB 6:14 ***"A despairing man should have the devotion of his friends,** even though he forsakes the fear of the Almighty.*

JOB 42:10-11 **After Job had prayed for his friends, the LORD made him prosperous again** and gave him twice as much as he had before.

PROV 17:9 He who covers over an offense promotes love, but **whoever repeats the matter separates close friends.**

PROV 19:4 **Wealth brings many friends,** but a poor man's friend deserts him.

PROV 22:24 **Do not make friends with a hot-tempered man,** do not associate with one easily angered,

PROV 27:17 **As iron sharpens iron, so one man sharpens another.**

DAN 2:18-19 **He urged them to plead for mercy from the God of heaven** concerning this mystery, **so that he and his friends might not be executed** with the rest of the wise men of Babylon.

LUKE 16:8-9 "The master commended the dishonest manager because he had acted shrewdly. For the people of this world are more shrewd in dealing with their own kind than are the people of the light. **I tell you, use worldly wealth to gain friends for yourselves,** so that when it is gone, you will be welcomed into eternal dwellings.

JOHN 15:13-17 **Greater love has no one than this, that he lay down his life for his friends.** You are my friends if you do what I command. I no longer call you servants, because a servant does not know his master's business. Instead, I have called you friends, for everything that I learned from my Father I have made known to you. You did not choose me, but I chose you and appointed you to go and bear fruit-fruit that will last. Then the Father will give you whatever you ask in my name.

JUDE 20-21 But you, dear **friends, build yourselves up in your most holy faith and pray in the Holy Spirit.** Keep yourselves in God's love as you wait for the mercy of our Lord Jesus Christ to bring you to eternal life.

PHYSICAL ATTRIBUTE ADVANTAGES OF FRIENDS: Multiplies Companion Perception Options.

WITHOUT IT: Verifies my selfishness.

WITH IT: Verifies my discovery of intangible resource tools; love, forgiveness, faith, etc that enhances my life experience.

FOR COUPLE/GROUP:

Blood of Jesus Christ on our FRIENDS so that the Word of God can Create Faithful Companions in our relationship/s.

Blood of Jesus Christ on my:

NEIGHBORHOOD so that the Word of God can Create Groups of Faithful Friends in my life.

REFERENCES:

EXO 20:17 *"You shall not covet your neighbor's house. You shall not covet your neighbor's wife, or his manservant or maidservant, his ox or donkey, or anything that belongs to your neighbor."*

DEUT 24:10-13 *When you make a loan of any kind to your neighbor, do not go into his house to get what he is offering as a pledge. Stay outside and let the man to whom you are making the loan bring the pledge out to you. If the man is poor, do not go to sleep with his pledge in your possession. Return his cloak to him by sunset so that he may sleep in it. Then he will thank you, and it will be regarded as a righteous act in the sight of the LORD your God.*

PROV 3:29 *Do not plot harm against your neighbor, who lives trustfully near you.*

PROV 26:18-19 *Like a madman shooting firebrands or deadly arrows is a man who deceives his neighbor and says, "I was only joking!"*

PROV 27:10 *Do not forsake your friend and the friend of your father, and do not go to your brother's house when disaster strikes you — better a neighbor nearby than a brother far away.*

MIC 7:5 *Do not trust a neighbor; put no confidence in a friend. Even with her who lies in your embrace be careful of your words.*

MATT 22:37-40 *Jesus replied: "'Love the Lord your God with all your heart and with all your soul and with all your mind.' This is the first and greatest commandment. And the second is like it: 'Love your neighbor as yourself.' All the Law and the Prophets hang on these two commandments."*

GAL 5:14-15 *The entire law is summed up in a single command: "Love your neighbor as yourself." If you keep on biting and devouring each other, watch out or you will be destroyed by each other.*

PHYSICAL ATTRIBUTE ADVANTAGES OF NEIGHBORHOOD:
Multiplies Security Perception Options.

WITHOUT IT: Verifies how I rely on intimidation to cover up my lack of good people interaction skills.

WITH IT: Verifies my development of multiple ways to communicate patience, comfort and companionship.

FOR COUPLE/GROUP:
Blood of Jesus Christ on our NEIGHBORHOOD so that the Word of God can Create Groups of Faithful Friends in our relationship/s.

Blood of Jesus Christ on my:
COMMUNITY so that the Word of God can Create Faithful Independent Autonomy in my life.

REFERENCES:

GEN 35:11-12 *And God said, "I am God Almighty; be fruitful and increase in number. A nation and **a community of nations will come from you,** and kings will come from your body.*

NUM 10:1-4 *The LORD said to Moses: **"Make two trumpets of hammered silver, and use them for calling the community together** and for having the camps set out. When both are sounded, the whole community is to assemble before you at the entrance to the Tent of Meeting.*

NUM14:1-2 *That night **all the people of the community raised their voices and wept aloud.***

NUM 14:36-38 *So the men Moses had sent to explore the land, who returned and made **the whole community grumble against him by spreading a bad report about it** — these men responsible for spreading the bad report about the land were struck down and died of a plague before the LORD. Of the men who went to explore the land, only Joshua son of Nun and Caleb son of Jephunneh survived.*

NUM 15:15-16 ***The community is to have the same rules for you and for the alien living among you;** this is a lasting ordinance for the generations to come. You and the alien shall be the same before the LORD:*

NUM 27:15-17 *Moses said to the LORD, "May the LORD, the God of the spirits of all mankind, **appoint a man over this community to go** out and come in before them, **one who will lead them** out and bring them in, **so the LORD's people will not be like sheep without a shepherd."***

JER 30:20 *Their children will be as in days of old, and **their community will be established before me;** I will punish all who oppress them.*

PHYSICAL ATTRIBUTE ADVANTAGES OF COMMUNITY: Multiplies Sustaining Perception Options.

WITHOUT IT: False paradigms about personal hierarchies plague my mind. Shy away from personal accountability.

WITH IT: Understand the long term positive effects of personal relationships. Embrace personal relationships. Feelings of integrity.

FOR COUPLE/GROUP:

Blood of Jesus Christ on our COMMUNITY so that the Word of God can Create Faithful Independent Autonomy in our relationship/s.

Blood of Jesus Christ on my:

CITY so that the Word of God can Create Faithful Local Alliances in my life.

REFERENCES:

GEN 11:4-9 *Then they said, "Come, let us build ourselves a city, with a tower that reaches to the heavens, so that we may make a name for ourselves and not be scattered over the face of the whole earth." But the LORD came down to see the city and the tower that the men were building. The LORD said, "If as one people speaking the same language they have begun to do this, then nothing they plan to do will be impossible for them. Come, let us go down and confuse their language so they will not understand each other." So the LORD scattered them from there over all the earth, and they stopped building the city.*

GEN 18:28 *what if the number of the righteous is five less than fifty? Will you destroy the whole city because of five people?" "If I find forty-five there," he said, "I will not destroy it."*

DEUT 28:3 *You will be blessed in the city and blessed in the country.*

PSALM 127:1 *Unless the LORD builds the house, its builders labor in vain. Unless the LORD watches over the city, the watchmen stand guard in vain.*

PROV 11:10-11 *When the righteous prosper, the city rejoices; when the wicked perish, there are shouts of joy. Through the blessing of the upright a city is exalted, but by the mouth of the wicked it is destroyed.*

PROV 18:11 *The wealth of the rich is their fortified city; they imagine it an unscalable wall.*

PROV 18:19 *An offended brother is more unyielding than a fortified city, and disputes are like the barred gates of a citadel.*

PROV 29:8 *Mockers stir up a city, but wise men turn away anger.*

ECCL 7:19 *Wisdom makes one wise man more powerful than ten rulers in a city.*

ECCL 9:15-16 *Now there lived in that city a man poor but wise, and **he saved the city by his wisdom.** But nobody remembered that poor man. So I said, **"Wisdom is better than strength."** But the poor man's wisdom is despised, and his words are no longer heeded.*

HAB 2:12 **"Woe to him who builds a city with bloodshed and establishes a town by crime!**

MATT 12:25-26 *Jesus knew their thoughts and said to them, "Every kingdom divided against itself will be ruined, and **every city or household divided against itself will not stand.***

PHYSICAL ATTRIBUTE ADVANTAGES OF CITY: Multiplies Local Alliance Perception Options.

WITHOUT IT: False paradigms about social hierarchies plague my mind. Shy away from social accountability. Feelings of betrayal.

WITH IT: Understand the long term positive effects of social relationships. Embrace social relationships. Feelings of trust.

FOR COUPLE/GROUP:
Blood of Jesus Christ on our CITY so that the Word of God can Create Faithful Local Alliances in our relationship/s.

Blood of Jesus Christ on my:
STATE so that the Word of God can Create Faithful Independent Alliances in my life.

REFERENCES:

GEN 32:9-11 *Then Jacob prayed, "O God of my father Abraham, God of my father Isaac, O LORD, who said to me, **'Go back to your country and your relatives, and I will make you prosper,'** I am unworthy of all the kindness and faithfulness you have shown your servant. I had only my staff when I crossed this Jordan, but now I have become two groups.*

GEN 41:36 **This food should be held in reserve for the country,** *to be used during the seven years of famine that will come upon Egypt, **so that the country may not be ruined by the famine."***

LEV 26:6-8 **"'I will grant peace in the land, and you will lie down and no one will make you afraid. I will remove savage beasts from the land, and the sword will not pass through your country.** *You will pursue your enemies, and they will fall by the sword before you. Five of you will chase a hundred, and* a hundred of you will chase ten thousand, and your enemies will fall by the sword before you.

JOSH 2:8-10 Before the spies lay down for the night, she went up on the roof and said to them, "I know that the LORD has given this land to you and that a great fear of you has fallen on us, so that **all who live in this country are melting in fear because of you.**

PROV 28:2 **When a country is rebellious, it has many rulers,** but a man of understanding and knowledge maintains order.

PROV 29:4 **By justice a king gives a country stability,** but one who is greedy for bribes tears it down.

JOHN 4:44-45 Now Jesus himself had pointed out that **a prophet has no honor in his own country.**

HEB 11:9-10 **By faith he made his home in the promised land like a stranger in a foreign country;** he lived in tents, as did Isaac and Jacob, who were heirs with him of the same promise. For he was looking forward to the city with foundations, whose architect and builder is God.

PHYSICAL ATTRIBUTE ADVANTAGES OF STATE: Multiples Independent Alliance Perception Options.

WITHOUT IT: False paradigms about organization hierarchies plague my mind. Shy away from organization accountability. Feelings of abandonment.

WITH IT: Understand the long term positive effects of organization relationships. Embrace organization relationships. Feelings of belonging.

FOR COUPLE/GROUP:
Blood of Jesus Christ on our STATE so that the Word of God can Create Faithful Independent Alliances in our relationship/s.

Blood of Jesus Christ on my:
NATION so that the Word of God can Create Faithful Nations/ Alliances from My Lyons in my life.

REFERENCES:

GEN 12:2-3 *"I will make you into a great nation and I will bless you; I will make your name great, and you will be a blessing. 3* I will bless those who bless you, and whoever curses you I will curse; and *all peoples on earth will be blessed through you."*

GEN 35:11-12 And God said to him, "I am God Almighty; be fruitful and increase in number. *A nation and a community of nations will come from you, and kings will come from your body.*

PSLAM 33:12 *Blessed is the nation whose God is the LORD,* the people he chose for his inheritance.

PROV 11:14 *For lack of guidance a nation falls,* but many advisers make victory sure.

ISAIAH 2:4 He will judge between the nations and will settle disputes for many peoples. They will beat their swords into plowshares and their spears into pruning hooks. *Nation will not take up sword against nation, nor will they train for war anymore.*

ISAIAH 60:22 *The least of you will become* a thousand, the smallest *a mighty nation.* I am the LORD; in its time I will do this swiftly."

ISAIAH 66:8 Who has ever heard of such a thing? Who has ever seen such things? *Can a country be born in a day or a nation be brought forth in a moment?*

Yet no sooner is Zion in labor than she gives birth to her children.

1 PETER 2:9-10 But *you are a chosen people, a royal priesthood, a holy nation,* a people belonging to God, that you may declare the praises of him who called you out of darkness into his wonderful light. Once you were not a people, but now you are the people of God; once you had not received mercy, but now you have received mercy.

PHYSICAL ATTRIBUTE ADVANTAGES OF NATION: Multiplies Multiple Common Independent Alliances Perception Options.

WITHOUT IT: False paradigms about domestic hierarchies plague my mind. Shy away from domestic accountability. Feelings of antiarchy.

WITH IT: Understand the long term positive effects of domestic relationships. Embrace domestic relationships. Feelings of peace.

FOR COUPLE/GROUP:

Blood of Jesus Christ on our NATION so that the Word of God can Create Faithful Nations/Alliances from Our Lyons in our relationship/s.

Blood of Jesus Christ on my:

WORLD so that the Word of God can Create International Faithful Alliances in my life.

REFERENCES:

GEN 11:1-7 ***Now the whole world had one language and a common speech.*** *As men moved eastward, they found a plain in Shinar and settled there. They said to each other, "Come, let's make bricks and bake them thoroughly." They used brick instead of stone, and tar for mortar. Then they said, "Come, let us build ourselves a city, with a tower that reaches to the heavens, so that we may make a name for ourselves and not be scattered over the face of the whole earth." But the LORD came down to see the city and the tower that the men were building. The LORD said, **"If as one people speaking the same language they have begun to do this, then nothing they plan to do will be impossible for them.**

1 SAM 2:8-9 *He raises the poor from the dust and lifts the needy from the ash heap; he seats them with princes and has them inherit a throne of honor. **"For the foundations of the earth are the LORD's; upon them he has set the world.** He will guard the feet of his saints, but the wicked will be silenced in darkness. "It is not by strength that one prevails;*

1 CHRON 16:30 *Tremble before him, all the earth!* **The world is firmly established; it cannot be moved.**

DAN 4:1-3 *King Nebuchadnezzar, **to the peoples, nations and men of every language, who live in all the world: May you prosper greatly!** It is my pleasure to tell you about the miraculous signs and wonders that the Most High God has performed for me. How great are his signs, how mighty his wonders! His kingdom is an eternal kingdom; his dominion endures from generation to generation.*

JOHN 3:16-17 **"For God so loved the world that he gave his one and only Son,** *that whoever believes in him shall not perish but have eternal life. For **God did not send his Son into the world to condemn the world, but to save the world through him.***

JOHN 12:30-32 *Jesus said, "This voice was for your benefit, not mine. Now is the time for judgment on this world; **now the prince of this world will be driven out.***

PHYSICAL ATTRIBUTE ADVANTAGES OF WORLD: Multiplies Multiple Uncommon Independent Alliances Perception Options.

WITHOUT IT: False paradigms about foreign hierarchies plague my mind. Shy away from foreign accountability. Feelings of isolation.

WITH IT: Understand the long term positive effects of foreign relationships. Embrace foreign relationships. Feelings of order.

FOR COUPLE/GROUP:

Blood of Jesus Christ on our WORLD so that the Word of God can Create International Faithful Alliances in our relationship/s.

Blood of Jesus Christ on my:

UNIVERSE so that the Word of God can be In My All, Through My All and With My All in my life.

REFERENCES:

1 COR 4:9-13 *For it seems to me that God has put us apostles on display at the end of the procession, like men condemned to die in the arena.* **We have been made a spectacle to the whole universe, to angels as well as to men.** *We are fools for Christ, but you are so wise in Christ! We are weak, but you are strong! You are honored, we are dishonored! To this very hour we go hungry and thirsty, we are in rags, we are brutally treated, we are homeless. We work hard with our own hands. When we are cursed, we bless; when we are persecuted, we endure it; when we are slandered, we answer kindly. Up to this moment we have become the scum of the earth, the refuse of the world.*

EPH 4:10 **He who descended is the very one who ascended higher than all the heavens, in order to fill the whole universe.**

HEB 1:1-4 *In the past God spoke to our forefathers through the prophets at many times and in various ways, but* **in these last days he has spoken to us by his Son, whom he appointed heir of all things, and through whom he made the universe. The Son is the radiance of God's glory and the exact representation of his being, sustaining all things by his powerful word.** *After he had provided purification for sins, he sat down at the right hand of the Majesty in heaven. So he became as much superior to the angels as the name he has inherited is superior to theirs.*

HEB 11:3 **By faith we understand that the universe was formed at God's command, so that what is seen was not made out of what was visible.**

PHYSICAL ATTRIBUTE ADVANTAGES OF UNIVERSE: Infinite Multi-Dimensional Perception Options.

WITHOUT IT: False paradigms about origin of life hierarchies plague my mind. Shy away from origin of life accountability. Feelings of chaos.

WITH IT: Understand the long term positive effects of eternal truths. Embrace eternal truths. Feelings of destiny.

FOR COUPLE/GROUP:

Blood of Jesus Christ on our UNIVERSES so that the Word of God can be In Our All, Through Our All and With Our All in our relationship/s.

Here's the kicker.

Blood of Jesus Christ on my:

TESTIMONY so that the Word of God can be Manifested and Established as Eternal and True in, with and through my life.

REFERENCES:

EXO 23:2-3 *"Do not follow the crowd in doing wrong.* **When you give testimony in a lawsuit, do not pervert justice by siding with the crowd,** *and do not show favoritism to a poor man in his lawsuit.*

EXO 30:6 **Put the altar in front of the curtain** *that is before the ark of the Testimony —* **before** *the atonement cover that is over* **the Testimony — where I will meet with you.**

EXO 34:29 **When Moses came down** *from Mount Sinai* **with the two tablets of the Testimony in his hands, he was not aware that his face was radiant** *because he had spoken with the LORD.*

DEUT 19:15 *One witness is not enough to convict a man accused of any crime or offense he may have committed.* **A matter must be established by the testimony of two or three witnesses.**

PROV 25:18 **Like a club or a sword or a sharp arrow is the man who gives false testimony against his neighbor.**

ISAIAH 29:21 *those who with a word make a man out to be guilty, who ensnare the defender in court and* **with false testimony deprive the innocent of justice.**

JOHN 5:31 **"If I testify about myself, my testimony is not valid.**

1 COR 1:6-7 **because our testimony about Christ was confirmed in you.**

REV 12:11 **They overcame him by the blood of the Lamb and by the word of their testimony;** *they did not love their lives so much as to shrink from death.*

FOR COUPLE/GROUP:
Blood of Jesus Christ on our TESTIMONY so that the Word of God can be Manifested and Established as Eternal and True in, with and through the Life in our relationship/s.

And now for the final slam dunk. Combos.

Blood of Jesus Christ on my:
BLOOD AND TESTIMONY so that the Word of God can be Perpetuately Manifested and Established as Eternally True in, with and through my life.

REFERENCES:
We over came the devil/divider of the brethen/self-centerism by the blood of the lamb and our testimony. Is somebody prorogating slander against you. This will shut them down.

REV 12:11 **They overcame him by the blood of the Lamb and by the word of their testimony;** *they did not love their lives so much as to shrink from death.*

REV 17:6 *I saw that the woman was drunk with the blood of the saints,* **the blood of those who bore testimony to Jesus.**

FOR COUPLE/GROUP:
Blood of Jesus Christ on our BLOOD AND TESTIMONY so that the Word of God can be Perpetuately Manifested and Established as Eternally True in, with and through the life in our relationship/s.

Your twisting my arm. Ok. *Stop it.* One more and then I got to get this book published. Here's one more combo example.

Blood of Jesus Christ on my:

TESTIMONY, HONOR AND LIABILITIES so that the Word of God can be Manifested and Established as Eternally True, Glorified and Quenching my Thrist in, with and through my life.

FOR COUPLE/GROUP:

Blood of Jesus Christ on our TESTIMONY, HONOR AND LIABILITIES so that the Word of God can be Manifested and Established as Eternally True, Glorified and Quenching our Thrist in, with and through the life in our relationship/s.

Application

If we continue to address our enemies like the world does then we'll get a life full of hypocrisy, chaos, loneliness and death.

ROM 8:6-7. *The mind of sinful man is death,*

but the mind controlled by the Spirit is life and peace;

However, if we want a life with a peace that passes all understanding

PHIL 4:7. *And **the peace of God, which transcends all understanding, will guard your hearts and your minds in Christ Jesus.***

then we'll need to engage the Holy Spirit, in the battle of life and death over our minds and hearts. If we continue to address our enemies with the renewing of our minds

ROM 12:2. *Do not conform any longer to the pattern of this world, **but be transformed by the renewing of your mind.** Then you will be able to test and approve what God's will is-his good, pleasing and perfect will.*

and take captive every thought

2 COR 10:5. *We demolish arguments and every pretension that sets itself up against the knowledge of God, and we **take captive every thought** to make it obedient to Christ.*

then we will have a life full of peace that passes all understanding, absolutes, life and friendships.

All new endeavors are awkward to start. They require a commitment from us to change our current perspective to a new desired perspective. The end result is a new lifestyle. A new outcome.

Maximizing the Armor of God manual,
gives us a deeper look into the options, at taking captive
the thoughts that come against us in our minds and then
subject them to the Word of God. Christ mention,

MATT 7:3-5. *"Why do you look at the speck of sawdust in your brother's eye and
pay no attention to the plank in your own eye? How can you say to your brother,
'Let me take the speck out of your eye,' when all the time there is a plank in your
own eye? You hypocrite, first **take the plank out of your own eye, and then you
will see clearly to remove the speck from your brother's eye.***

and Paul mentions,

1 COR 12:26. ***If one part suffers, every part suffers with it;***
if one part is honored, every part rejoices with it.

For those of us who need to deal with a specific area in
our lives that wasn't covered in this manual,
we can use the same format. Example:

The blood of Jesus Christ on my "*fill in blank*"
so that the Word of God can "*fill in blank*" in my life.

Analyze the good characteristics/attributes of the item
your covering the Blood of Jesus Christ on.
If there are more then one attribute, try to summarize
them with one or few words that will cover the attributes.

If you would like help doing this, please email us at
our website maximizingthearmorofgod.com

For areas outside our body; families, communities and
nations, we have four other books that address these
areas, *The Art of Spiritual Warfare,*
The Five Offices,
New Revelations on Revelations
And *The Kings in Christ's Kingdom.*

Maximizing the Armor of God manual along with four other books, make up a five book series. This series allows us to take the logistics of the Armor of God, that the Apostle Paul gives us, combined with harnessing our thoughts, to give us Impenetrable Spiritual Armor of God to the Nth Degree.

APPLICATION - PROCESS:
Scripture References that relate to our challenges in getting a hold of our thoughts.

ROM 5:1-5. *Therefore, since we have been justified through faith, we have peace with God through our Lord Jesus Christ, through whom we have gained access by faith into this grace in which we now stand. And we rejoice in the hope of the glory of God. Not only so, but we also rejoice in our sufferings, because we know that suffering produces perseverance; perseverance, character; and character, hope. And hope does not disappoint us, because God has poured out his love into our hearts by the Holy Spirit, whom he has given us.*

ROM 1:17B. *just as it is written: "The righteous will live by faith."*

JOHN 14:12-13. *I tell you the truth, anyone who has faith in me will do what I have been doing. He will do even greater things than these, because I am going to the Father.*

LUKE 17:6. *He replied, "If you have faith as small as a mustard seed, you can say to this mulberry tree, 'Be uprooted and planted in the sea,' and it will obey you.*

GAL 2:19-21. *I have been crucified with Christ and I no longer live, but Christ lives in me. The life I live in the body, I live by faith in the Son of God, who loved me and gave himself for me.*

ZECH 10:5. *Together they will be like mighty men trampling the muddy streets in battle. Because the LORD is with them, they will fight and overthrow the horsemen.*

2 COR 6:3-10. *We put no stumbling block in anyone's path, so that our ministry will not be discredited. Rather, as servants of God we commend ourselves in every way: in great endurance; in troubles, hardships and distresses; in beatings, imprisonments and riots; in hard work, sleepless nights and hunger; in purity, understanding, patience and kindness; in the Holy Spirit and in sincere love; in truthful speech and in the power of God; with weapons of righteousness in the right hand and in the left; through glory and dishonor, bad report and good report; genuine, yet regarded as impostors; known, yet regarded as unknown; dying, and yet we live on; beaten, and yet not killed; sorrowful, yet always*

rejoicing; poor, yet making many rich; having nothing, and yet possessing everything.

2 COR 10:2-6. *For though we live in the world, we do not wage war as the world does. The weapons we fight with are not the weapons of the world. On the contrary, they have divine power to demolish strongholds. We demolish arguments and every pretension that sets itself up against the knowledge of God, and we take captive every thought to make it obedient to Christ.*

LUKE 12:31. *But seek his kingdom, and these things will be given to you as well.*

MATT 10:37-39. *"Anyone who loves his father or mother more than me is not worthy of me; anyone who loves his son or daughter more than me is not worthy of me; and anyone who does not take his cross and follow me is not worthy of me. Whoever finds his life will lose it, and whoever loses his life for my sake will find it.*

LUKE 9:62. *Jesus replied, "No one who puts his hand to the plow and looks back is fit for service in the kingdom of God."*

1 COR 16:13-14. *Be on your guard; stand firm in the faith; be men of courage; be strong. Do everything in love.*

2 PET 1:5-9. *For this very reason, make every effort to add to your faith goodness; and to goodness, knowledge; and to knowledge, self-control; and to self-control, perseverance; and to perseverance, godliness; and to godliness, brotherly kindness; and to brotherly kindness, love. For if you possess these qualities in increasing measure, they will keep you from being ineffective and unproductive in your knowledge of our Lord Jesus Christ. But if anyone does not have them, he is nearsighted and blind, and has forgotten that he has been cleansed from his past sins.*

JER 33:3-4. *'Call to me and I will answer you and tell you great and unsearchable things you do not know.'*

MATT 21:22. *And all things, whatsoever ye shall ask in prayer, believing, ye shall receive.*

JOHN 14:13. *And whatsoever ye shall ask in my name, that will I do, that the Father may be glorified in the Son. KJV*

ISAIAH 45:11. *Thus saith the LORD, the Holy One of Israel, and his Maker, Ask me of things to come concerning my sons, and concerning the work of my hands command ye me. KJV*

JAMES: 1:2-4. *Consider it pure joy, my brothers, whenever you face trails of many kinds, because you know that the testing of your faith develops perseverance. Perseverance must finish its work so that you may be mature and complete, not lacking anything.*

PSALM 91:15. *He will call upon me, and I will answer him; I will be with him in trouble, I will deliver him and honor him.*

David had many victories but in 1 SAM 30:1-8 there was no victory, the enemy held their wives and children captive. He wept until he could weep no more, then in verse six, David encourages himself in the Lord, his God.

There will be times when, we make a break through in our taking captive our thoughts and no one around us will give a rip.
We will have to. We will have to do something different to motivate ourselves, like start dancing when nobody else is.

APPLICATION -
SPIRITUAL VERBAL BATTLE EXAMPLE:
Scripture Reference on Satan's Verbal Battle with Christ.

MATT 4:1-11. *Then Jesus was led by the Spirit into the desert to be tempted by the devil. After fasting forty days and forty nights, he was hungry.*

We might not be led to fast for forty days and nights, but we've had events in our lives, that have push us to our limits and beyond. It's in these moments, we either give in or hang on. Other than a God intervention moment, our fates will be determined on the protection we chose, how much we practiced with it and how well we can use it. Our choice of weapon is God's Word. So death comes into our lives either to mess it up or kick us when we're down.

The tempter came to him and said, "If you are the Son of God, tell these stones to become bread." Jesus answered, "It is written: 'Man does not live on bread alone, but on every word that comes from the mouth of God.'"

Life and death are in the power of the tongue they that love it will eat the fruit there of. PROV 18:21. With this in mind, we personalize this with something like, "We shall not live by bread alone but by the Word of God that

proceedeth out of our mouths". Hypocrisy? No. Because
faith come by hearing the word. ROM 10:17. To increase
and strengthen our faith we need to hear it. A lot. A whole
bunch. And then test it a lot. Over and over.
Without out faith we can not please God. HEB 11:6.
If we grasp this or not, death keeps coming back -
until his locked up for thousand years,
to call our bluffs, guaranteed. ACTS 19:15.

*Then the devil took him to the holy city and had him stand on the highest
point of the temple. "If you are the Son of God," he said, "throw yourself
down. For it is written: "'He will command his angels concerning you, and
they will lift you up in their hands, so that you will not strike your foot
against a stone.'" Jesus answered him, "It is also written: 'Do not put the Lord
your God to the test.'"*

What comes to mind here, is a couple of issues. One, the
devil is tempting Christ (God in the Flesh) to misuse/abuse
His authoritative position. Bitterly suggesting Christ (God
in the Flesh) to mock or toy with His relationship with God
the Father and the angels. Two, this reveals how and what
the devil thought and acted before his fallen state. With
this in mind, we can personalize this something like, "Just
because we are the children of God doesn't mean we have
to prove it to you devil by jeopardizing our relationship
with our loved ones."

*Again, the devil took him to a very high mountain and showed him all the
kingdoms of the world and their splendor. "All this I will give you," he said,
"if you will bow down and worship me." Jesus said to him, "Away from me,
Satan! For it is written: 'Worship the Lord your God, and serve him only.'"
Then the devil left him, and angels came and attended him.*

Afterwards the devil fled and the angels came and
this could have been a really tough verbal encounter but
I'm thinking that was just too easy. A few words were
exchanged and the tempter doesn't even debate back. It
seems like he would of at least brought out his hordes and

tried to trash Christ. Some how. It would have been a good
time to take advantage of Him. Christ is suppose to be
worn out, right? Forty days without food? That's got to be a
tough one to pull off? Only if we think about it in terms of
our limitations. Remember, Christ can't die until the
appointed time. He could of fasted 120 days.
It doesn't matter. He's God in the flesh!

Since the tempter didn't debate back, this indicates - it
doesn't take much of God's Word to scare him off.
And since the tempter didn't bring out his hordes,
this indicates he doesn't have enough confidence in his
fallen angels to pull off a coup.

Now after he wimps out, the angels came and ministered
to Christ. We didn't check the Hebrew/Greek on this
one. But Webster indicates *minister* in respect to religion
means, "to give aid or service." How can anyone attend,
give aid or service to God in the flesh-Christ. No one can.
God is everything to Himself. What seems more believable
is the
Angels came and ate with Christ. A Kingly Banquet in the
wilderness would be more fitting after a 40 day fast,
rather than a pity party.

If ministering is implying Christ suffered from mental
weakness, because of the lack of food and the experience,
then the devil appears to be stronger than Christ.
But this contradicts when Christ resist the thoughts of
avoiding His Father's will in the garden of Gethsemane.
A few hours one night compared to forty days and nights
without food. Which is tougher?

Avoiding food for forty days or avoiding the Cross?
Yah. The Cross is tougher. Whereas the Devil flees Christ

after Christ speaks three statements. Hmm.
With all this in mind, we can personalize it with
something like, "Hmm. No thank you. We're co-heirs
with Christ Jesus already. And a matter fact, we're ruling
with Him as Kings and Priest."

APPLICATION - EXAMPLE SUMMARY:

Christ puts the Devil in his place. - Man will live by My
Words, not by your bread. You - Devil - shall not tempt me.
I am your Lord and God, who made you - not you, me.
You - Devil - are to worship and
serve Me - your God.

This makes more sense why the tempter cuts his
conversation short and escapes while he could.

APPLICATION - END RESULTS:
Scripture References that relate to our victories in overcoming our challenges - for getting a hold of our thoughts.

ISAIAH 41:9-13. *I took you from the ends of the earth, from its farthest corners I called you. I said, 'You are my servant'; I have chosen you and have not rejected you. So do not fear, for I am with you; do not be dismayed, for I am your God. I will strengthen you and help you; I will uphold you with my righteous right hand. "All who rage against you will surely be ashamed and disgraced; those who oppose you will be as nothing and perish. Though you search for your enemies, you will not find them. Those who wage war against you will be as nothing at all. For I am the LORD, your God, who takes hold of your right hand and says to you, Do not fear; I will help you.*

MATT 19:29-30. *And everyone who has left houses or brothers or sisters or father or mother or children or fields for my sake will receive a hundred times as much and will inherit eternal life.*

PROV 29:2. *When the righteous are in authority, the people rejoice; but when a wicked man rules, the people groan NKJV.*

PROV 11:10. *When the righteous prosper, the city rejoices; when the wicked perish, there are shouts of joy.*

PROV 28:12. *When the righteous triumph, there is great elation; but when the wicked rise to power, men go into hiding.*

EPH 3:16-21. *I pray that out of his glorious riches he may strengthen you with power through his Spirit in your inner being, so that Christ may dwell in your hearts through faith. And I pray that you, being rooted and established in love, may have power, together with all the saints, to grasp how wide and long and high and deep is the love of Christ, and to know this love that surpasses knowledge that you may be filled to the measure of all the fullness of God. Now to him who is able to do immeasurably more than all we ask or imagine, according to his power that is at work within us,to him be glory in the church and in Christ Jesus throughout all generations, for ever and ever! Amen.*

LUKE 19:13. *And he called his ten servants, and delivered them ten pounds, and said unto them, Occupy till I come. KJV*

GAL 3:26-27. *You are all sons of God through faith in Christ Jesus, for all of you who were baptized into Christ have clothed yourselves with Christ.*

1 JOHN 5:4-5. *for everyone born of God overcomes the world. This is the victory that has overcome the world, even our faith. Who is it that overcomes the world? Only he who believes that Jesus is the Son of God.*

JOEL 2:25. *"So I will restore to you the years that the swarming locust has eaten, The crawling locust, The consuming locust, And the chewing locust, My great army which I sent among you. NKJV*

DEUT 28:8. *The LORD shall command the blessing upon thee in thy storehouses, and in all that thou settest thine hand unto; and he shall bless thee in the land which the LORD thy God giveth thee. KJV*

JOEL 2:25. *'I will repay you for the years the locusts have eaten- the great locust and the young locust, the other locusts and the locust swarm-*

PSALMS 112:1-3. *Praise the LORD. Blessed is the man who fears the LORD, who finds great delight in his commands. His children will be mighty in the land; the generation of the upright will be blessed. Wealth and riches are in his house, and his righteousness endures forever.*

DEUT 28:1-2. *And all these blessings shall come upon you and overtake you, because you obey the voice of the LORD your God: NKJV*

DEUT 28:12-13. *The LORD will open to you His good treasure, the heavens, to give the rain to your land in its season, and to bless all the work of your hand. You shall lend to many nations, but you shall not borrow. NKJV*

PROV 29:2. *When the righteous are in authority, the people rejoice; but when a wicked man rules, the people groan NKJV.*

MARK 16:16-18. *Whoever believes and is baptized will be saved, but whoever does not believe will be condemned. And these signs will accompany those who believe: In my name they will drive out demons; they will speak in new tongues; they will pick up snakes with their hands; and when they drink deadly poison, it will not hurt them at all; they will place their hands on sick people, and they will get well."*

APPLICATION - IF NOT FOR OURSELVES THEN FOR OUR LOVED ONES:
Scripture References for Considering Our Future Generations and Legacies.

ISAIAH 44:3-5. *For I will pour water on the thirsty land, and streams on the dry ground; I will pour out my Spirit on your offspring, and my blessing on your descendants. They will spring up like grass in a meadow, like poplar trees by flowing streams. One will say, 'I belong to the LORD'; another will call himself by the name of Jacob; still another will write on his hand,*

> *'The LORD's,' and will take the name Israel.*

Consider

Our unseen enemies clearly understand they must first wear down our mental lives, before they can destroy our mental, physical and spiritual lives. Once our enemies find out we're not mentally strong enough to handle/weather a conflict; we don't know who we are in Christ, we don't know how to stand on God's Word until we have a victory over our conflicts, we don't have the tenacity/perseverance to the point of death, we believe our enemies propaganda on how strong they are over God's Word, then our enemies will attack us verbally, physically and spiritually. Our enemies will wear us down, little by little, to the point we become verbal, physical and spiritual basket cases. Defeated. Isolated. Trapped. Hopeless and full of fear. When we understand this, we realize it's not the armor on the outside of our bodies that protects us or delivers us and or our loved ones, it's the strengthening of our inner armor, that has a more profound impact, on conquering our enemies. It's tearing down all the false paradigms/doctrines inside our minds, that we've believed as the truth. Once we begin conquering our enemies – false truths, our enemies don't have a chance in hell at defeating us. We turn the table against our enemies. We track them down. We torment our enemies, day and night, to the point, our enemies beg God to be thrown into the lake of fire, before it's their time. We become the Sons and Daughters of God, in the image of Christ. Now the gates of hell can't even hold us back. This is the cross roads we all face. We must make the decision that all of our battles in our lives, are either outside our bodies or inside our bodies. If we chose to believe, that the battles of our lives are on the outside our bodies then how do we process our experiences, in the darkness of our worlds, to the point of having victory over them. When others have not been able to conquer this, on their own, since the fall of man? Do we keep doing what the Body of Christ has been doing for the last two thousand years and expect different results? If we chose to believe that the battles of our lives are on the inside our bodies then how do we process our experiences in the darkness of our worlds, to the point of having victory over them?

We believe *Maximizing the Armor of God* is a new, out of the box approach, that assists us in conquering our thoughts, by putting the Blood of Christ on each function of our lives, to set them free. Once they are free, with the Holy Spirit, God will reveal to us, how we can strengthen who we are in Christ, in every part of our lives. The stronger we become, the weaker our enemies become at destroying us and our loved ones. Remember, we are caught between the Battle of the Warrior of Life and the Warrior of Death, warring over our souls, inside our minds. Which side will win? Which side will we chose? Death? Then do nothing and we will surely die. Life? Then let's enlist ourselves into the boot camp of learning, on how to conquer our enemies, by conquering who we are in Christ, by His Blood, in every part of our minds, souls and spirits.

W arrior's Advice

1. Our loved ones will be expecting compassion from us, as we lead and protect them. Those who have compassion will lead them ISAIAH 49:3-11. If we haven't had a sober near death experience or direct Christ encountered then more than likely, our compassion level is next to zero. We have more opinions then we do thoughts of compassion.

2. God goes out of His way, to make sure He gets all of the Proper Recognition/Glory, on Who really made it all happen. He doesn't let time, circumstances and emotions motivated Him for any reason. So the sooner we give Him all the glory publicly, the better off we'll be, in our time of testing. PROV 27:21.

3. Patience is the key in routing out our enemies.

    DEUT 7:21-24. *The LORD your God will drive out those nations before you, little by little. You will not be allowed to eliminate them all at once, or the wild animals will multiply around you. But the LORD your God will deliver them over to you, throwing them into great confusion until they are destroyed.*

    EXO 23:29-30. *I will not drive them out from before thee in one year; lest the land become desolate and the beast of the field multiply against thee. By little and little I will drive them out from before thee, **until thou be increased, and inherit** the land. KJV. **Note: When we increase at applying His Word to our lives, we increase at inheriting its manifestation.***

4. It's best to come to grips, real fast, it's just ourselves and Christ. Loved ones, friends and teams are comforting but they should never substitute the responsible relationship I need in Christ. A real relationship with Christ generates real peace in my life and with my loved ones.

2 TIM 4:16-18. *At my first defense, no one came to my support, but everyone deserted me. May it not be held against them. But the Lord stood at my side and gave me strength, so that through me the message might be fully proclaimed and all the Gentiles might hear it. And I was delivered from the lion's mouth. The Lord will rescue me from every evil attack and will bring me safely to his heavenly kingdom. To him be glory for ever and ever. Amen.*

Warrior's Mindset

COMPILATION OF PSALMS 23 USING THE
WORDS FAITH AND FEAR.

⛦THE FAITH PSALM⛦

1 – THE LORD IS MY SHEPARD
I SHALL NOT FEAR.

2 – HE MAKES ME TO LIE DOWN
IN GREEN PASTURES OF FAITH:
HE LEADS ME BESIDE
THE STILL WATERS OF FAITH.

3 – HE RESTORES MY FAITH:
HE LEADS ME IN THE PATHS OF FAITH
FOR HIS NAME'S SAKE.

4 – YEA, THOUGH I WALK
THROUGH THE VALLEY OF THE SHADOW OF FEAR,
I SHALL NOT FEAR:
FOR YOU ARE WITH ME;
YOUR WORD AND YOUR FAITH
COMFORT ME.

5 – YOU PREPARE A BANQUET TABLE OF FAITH BEFORE
ME IN THE PRESENCE OF MY FEAR:
YOU ANNOINT MY HEAD WITH FAITH;
MY FAITH OVERFLOWS.

6 – SURELY FAITH'S GOODNESS AND MERCY
SHALL FOLLOW ME
ALL THE DAYS OF MY LIFE:
AND I WILL DWELL
IN THE LORD'S HOUSE OF FAITH
FOREVER.

Warrior's Creed

I am the son/daughter of the Living God. Gal 3:26.
I am Co-heir in Christ. Rom 8:17.
I Dwell in the Throne Room of God. Heb 4:16.
I have the Same Authority and Resources as Christ. John 14:12-14.
I am Above All Nations, Kingdoms, etc. Jer 1:9-10.
I am Invincible. Rom 8:31-39.

I am Secure. Psalms 112:8.
I am Mighty. Psalms 112:2.
I am Fearless. Psalms 112:7.
I am Steadfast. Psalms 112:7.
I am Never Shaken. Psalms 112:5.
I am Never Uprooted. Prov 10:30.
I Trust the Lord of Lords. Psalms 112:7.
My Eyes are Full of Triumph. Psalms 112:8.

I am Generous. Psalms 112:5.
I Bring Life. Mark 16:18.
I Give Gifts Freely. Psalms 112:9.
I Lend and Never Borrow. Deut 28:12.
I Live by Faith not by Sight. Rom 1:17b.
My Faith is Powerful and Effective. Luke 17:6.
I am Rooted and Established in Love. Eph 3:17.
I Conduct my Affairs with Justice. Psalms 112:5.
I Destroy All Self-Centered Thoughts. Isa 41:11.
I Have Overcomed the World by my Faith. 1 John 5:4.
I am always in Authority and Prosperous. Prov 11:10.
I am More than a Conqueror in Christ Jesus. Rom 8:37.
I Destroy all Weapons Formed Against me. Isaiah 54:17.
My Hands Fill my Storehouses in All Seasons. Deut 28:11-12.
I Know How to Use All God's Treasures. Luke 12:31.
I Drive Out All Rebellious and Self-Centered Thoughts. Mark 16:17.
I am Compassionate, Righteous Man who Aluminates. Psalms 112:4.
I Feed the Hungry, Cloth the Naked and Free the Captives. Matt 25:35-36.

I am Lifted High in Honor. Psalms 112:9.
I am Remembered Forever. Psalms 112:6.
My righteousness in Christ Endures Forever. Psalms 112:3.

Warrior's Song

PSALMS 91:1-16.

I will dwell in the shelter of the Most High
and will rest in the shadow of the Almighty.
I will say of the LORD, "He is my refuge and my fortress,
my God, in whom I trust."
Surely He will save me from the fowler's snare
and from the deadly pestilence.
He will cover me with His feathers,
and under His wings I will find refuge;
His faithfulness will be my shield and rampart.
I will not fear the terror of night,
nor the arrow that flies by day,
nor the pestilence that stalks in the darkness,
nor the plague that destroys at midday.
A thousand may fall at my side, ten thousand at my right hand,
death will not come near me.
I will only observe with my eyes
and see the punishment of the wicked.
I will make the Most High my dwelling
— even the LORD, who is my refuge —
no harm will befall me, no disaster will come near my tent.
For He will command His angels
concerning me to guard me in all my ways;
they will lift me up in their hands,
so that I will not strike my foot against a stone.
I will tread upon the lion and the cobra;
I will trample the great lion and the serpent.
"Because He loves me," says the LORD,
"I will rescue him; I will protect him,
for he acknowledges my name. He will call upon me,
and I will answer him; I will be with him in trouble,
I will deliver him and honor him.
With long life will I satisfy him
and show him my salvation."

Optimum Vizh-an

We thank You for all the goodness You are about to bestow
upon us again; with this good meal, good drink, good
times and good wealth,
for the soul purpose of Glorifying You better than before.

W<u>arrior's</u> Bl<u>essing</u>

Our wounds and scars have gotten the best of us.
Most of us could tell stories, that would leave the rest of
us awe stricken, at God's unfailing mercy and compassion.
Some of us haven't touched a day of peace or restoration,
in a real long time. **HOLD ON**. We're one day closer to
receiving what our Creator has promised us. Until then,
we're given hopes from God's Word, to share with one
another as encouragements, prayers and blessings.

*The God of peace will soon crush
Satan under our feet.
The grace of our Lord Jesus
be with us all.*
ROMANS 16:20.

*But the Lord is faithful,
and He will strengthen
and protect us
from the evil one.*
2 THES 3:2-4.

*The Spirit Himself testifies with our spirit
that we are God's children.
Now if we are children,
then we are heirs-heirs of God
and co-heirs with Christ,
if indeed we share in His sufferings
in order that we may also share
in His glory.*
ROMANS 8:15-17.

*Beloved, I pray that you may
prosper in all things and be in health,
just as your soul prospers.*
3 JOHN 2-3. NKJV

God richly bless you with wisdom, strength and
perseverance, in keeping His Word, for the benefit of
bringing restoration to you and your loved ones.

Index

E

EARS so that the Word of God can Receive the Faith Required in my life, 62

ELBOWS so that the Word of God can Labor in my life, 53

EYES so that the Word of God can Bring into View the Kingdom of God in my life, 68

F

FAITH so that the Word of God can Move Mountains in my life, 113

FAMILY so that the Word of God can Produce and Guide My Offspring in my life, 130

FAT so that the Word of God can Over Flow in my life, 82

FEET so that the Word of God can Stand Firm in my life, 36

FINANCES so that the Word of God can Create My Safe Haven in my life, 121

FINGERS so that the Word of God can Manifest God's Design Purpose in my life, 57

FOREHEAD so that the Word of God can Keep Moving Forward in my life, 60

FRIENDS so that the Word of God can Create Faithful Companions in my life, 131

H

Habakkuk, ix

HAIR so that the Word of God can be Adorned and Anointed in my life, 64

HANDS so that the Word of God can create God's Design Purpose in my life, 55

HEAD so that the Word of God can be Meditated on Day and Night in my life, 59

HEART so that the Word of God can be Treasured in my life, 83

HELMET OF SALVATION so that the Word of God can establish an Auto Thought Management System in my life, 108

HOME so that the Word of God can be a Safe Haven in my life, 124

HONOR so that the Word of God can be Glorified in my life, 117

HOPE so that the Word of God can Manifest Restoration in my life, 114

I

IMMUNE SYSTEM so that the Word of God can Resist in my life, 92

INCOME PRODUCING ENTITIES so that the Word of God can Reveal Creations Hidden Mysteries in my life, 122

INTEGRITY so that the Word of God can be Steadfast in my life, 118

INTESTINES so that the Word of God can be Absorbed in my life, 80

R

REPRODUCTIVE SYSTEM so that the Word of God can Multiply in my life, 93

RESPIRATORY SYSTEM so that the Word of God can Breath in my life, 91

REST so that the Word of God can create Complete Rest in my life, 96

RIGHT BIG TOE so that the Word of God will Keep Balanced in my life, 38

RIGHT EAR LOBE so that the Word of God can Manifest the Faith Required in my life, 61

RIGHT ELBOW so that the Word of God can be Leveraged Exponentially in my life, 53

RIGHT EYE so that the Word of God can Encourage in my life, 67

RIGHT KNEE so that the Word of God will Submit to the Father in my life, 40

RIGHT NOSTRIL so that the Word of God can be Discerned in my life, 70

RIGHT SHOULDER so that the Word of God can have Velocity in my life, 49

RIGHT THIGH so that the Word of God will Wrestle with God for a New Name in my life, 42

RIGHT THUMB so that the Word of God can Prosper in and for my life, 56

Romans, xiv

S

SHIELD OF FAITH so that the Word of God can establish an Auto Spiritual Defense System in my life, 107

SHOULDERS so that the Word of God can Accomplish the Required Task in my life, 50

SIDE so that the Word of God can Develop Relationships that Glorify God in my life, 46

SKILLS so that the Word of God can Protect My Safe Haven in my life, 119

SKIN so that the Word of God can Hold Together the Life in my life, 63

SOLES OF MY FEET so that the Word of God can Protect me From my Past and Walk me Through the Future Fires in my life, 35

SOUL so that the Word of God can be Resurrected in my life, 98

SPIRIT so that the Word of God can Save Me from Death in my life, 99

STANCE so that the Word of God can establish a Physical Position in my life, 110

STATE so that the Word of God can Create Faithful Independent Alliances in my life, 136

SWORD OF THE SPIRIT so that the Word of God can establish a Manual Spiritual Defense System in my life, 109